The People's Money

The People's Money

The Case for Public Banking in the United States

Adrian Kuzminski

LEXINGTON BOOKS
Lanham • Boulder • New York • London

Published by Lexington Books
An imprint of The Rowman & Littlefield Publishing Group, Inc.
4501 Forbes Boulevard, Suite 200, Lanham, Maryland 20706
www.rowman.com

86-90 Paul Street, London EC2A 4NE

British Library Cataloguing in Publication Information Available

Library of Congress Cataloging-in-Publication Data

Names: Kuzminski, Adrian, 1944- author.
Title: The people's money : the case for public banking in the United States / Adrian Kuzminski.
Description: Lanham : Lexington Books, [2024] | Includes bibliographical references and index.
Identifiers: LCCN 2023046369 (print) | LCCN 2023046370 (ebook) | ISBN 9781666949018 (cloth ; alk. paper) | ISBN 9781666949025 (epub)
Subjects: LCSH: Banks and banking--United States--History. | Populism--Economic aspects--United States--History.
Classification: LCC HG2461 .K89 2024 (print) | LCC HG2461 (ebook) | DDC 332.10973--dc23/eng/20231004
LC record available at https://lccn.loc.gov/2023046369
LC ebook record available at https://lccn.loc.gov/2023046370

∞™ The paper used in this publication meets the minimum requirements of American National Standard for Information Sciences—Permanence of Paper for Printed Library Materials, ANSI/NISO Z39.48-1992.

Contents

Acknowledgments

The following persons contributed in some unique way to the writing of this book: George McGuire, Phillip Mendlow, Paul Lebow, Lucille Eckrich, Joe Polito, Govert Schuler, Wayne Mellor, Antoinette Kuzminski, Alexandra Rallo, and an anonymous reader for Lexington Books. My thanks to each of them. For better or worse, however, I alone am responsible for the conclusions drawn in what follows.

Introduction

American populism was once a powerful, organized, radical mass movement. Its high point was the People's Party, a third party whose candidate for president in 1892, James B. Weaver, won over a million popular votes and twenty-two electoral votes. The party won eleven House seats, three senate seats, and several state governorships. This work, *The People's Money: The Prospect for Public Banking in the United States,* offers a broad account and analysis of the most radical policy proposal of the populist movement at its peak: a new monetary currency issued by a public banking system. It takes seriously populist monetary theory, long overlooked, as a precedent and template for future monetary reform.

To understand the central importance of monetary issues to American populists, it is necessary to recall the times in which they lived. The populism of the People's Party was the last stand of a deep-rooted Jeffersonian world of independent small producers, increasingly under threat from industrialization.[1] In contrast to the Old World they left, early America provided many European immigrants with an availability of resources for private ownership, relatively free of the constraints of aristocratic privilege and power. America early on became a land of small independent producers who governed themselves as democratically as they could, constrained as they were by the biases of their time (notably over race and slavery, women, and religion), and by the distant but real power of the British crown.

Their experience of rebelling from Great Britain left many Americans alert to new centralizing powers and disposed to resist them. The new powers they confronted appeared during and after the Civil War with the rise of large-scale industries (centered on railroads) and the financial system which funded them. The monopoly powers of private bankers in particular, as we shall see, created a monetary system which exploited smaller producers. This sparked, in reaction, the deepest articulation of Jeffersonian political economy: the American anti-monopoly populist movement of the late nineteenth century. A major (if neglected) contributor to populist thinking, central to this work, was

Edward Kellogg, who reflected the populist search for justice when he wrote, "Political Economy embraces the science and administration of law for securing to all their rights—that is, for securing to them the conditions requisite to the development of their various capabilities."[2] It was the 'conditions requisite' to securing the 'rights' of 'all' which the populists saw threatened, and which they resolved to defend.

Populism has proven hard to define. Today it seems to mean minimally an attitude of anti-elitism, mostly attributed to the grievances and resentments of the poorer, nativist, traditional, rural, white, conservative, working-class part of America. At its height as a movement, towards the end of the nineteenth century, populism primarily meant organized opposition to corporate monopolies. It was a movement first led by farmers in the South and West, and quickly joined by growing labor movements in the urban East and Midwest. This turned out to be an unsteady alliance which eventually fell apart under political pressure. The fault line within populism lay between capitalism and anti-capitalism, between small business people (including farmers), who owned (or aspired to own) the materials and means to produce goods and services for profit, and wage earners or workers who had no significant materials and means of production and were forced to sell their labor to live.

Up through the creation of the People's Party, anti-capitalist and even socialist sentiments were widely entertained in populist publications such as the *Farmers' Alliance*, which also called for price relief and easier credit for small businesspeople like farmers.[3] Rural farmers and urban factory workers were united in their anti-monopoly grievances, and both sides shared a labor theory of value. For the farmers the goal was to nationalize natural monopolies (like banks, railroads, and telegraph lines) in order to benefit, not hinder, capitalistic producers in non-monopolistic, mutually competing enterprises, of which farming was the most widespread. The workers, however, unlike farmers, lacking productive property, or capital, were inclined in their struggle for social justice to explore nationalizing not just natural monopolies, but *all* capitalist enterprises with an organized, industrial labor force of any significance at all. They saw little or no value in capitalism as such, which increasingly became the enemy. After their mutual electoral defeat in 1896, farmers and workers went their separate ways.

The populism addressed in this book comes out of the capitalist not the labor side of the movement. It explores the belief that small-scale capitalism—the widespread independent ownership of productive assets (means of production) among the people individually or as households—is essential to economic security and democratic government.[4] The freedom and courage to act as a citizen to help shape one's community was secured in the minds of capitalistic populists by the relative economic independence of citizen households. Although wealthy elites existed early on in America—mainly merchant traders and manufacturers in the commercial Northern cities, and large planters in the slaveholding South—most production and commerce in the antebellum era were otherwise widely distributed among sole proprietors operating on a family scale. Land was the principal asset for most producers, and farming the main unit of business activity, supported by largely local commercial and retail services: shop keepers, suppliers, mechanics, artisans, crafts people, inn keepers, and professionals (lawyers, doctors, officials, teachers, preachers, etc.). This was the world of decentralized local democracies and economies so eloquently described and made famous by Alexis de Tocqueville in his classic work, *Democracy in America*.[5]

Monetary issues were important to populists precisely because they themselves were capitalists. Let us define capitalism as the operation for a personal profit of some privately owned means of production. When your livelihood comes from running such an enterprise, even a small one, say a farm or a store or a repair shop, it is necessary in assessing one's business to calculate the rate of return on one's investment, or capital. In the modern commercial world already familiar to nineteenth century populist producers, needed capital was most commonly obtained as credit on a loan from a bank, the terms of which were often a make-or-break concern to the borrower. Capitalists small and large must take seriously the conditions of the issuance of money as debt by banks as the businesses they run often depend upon it. It can be their very lifeblood.

In the modern world, by contrast, the creation of money is confined to the opaque and arcane workings of corporate banks, central banks, and high finance. In the Jeffersonian-populist world, the producing capitalist classes dealt directly with their local private banks who created the money they needed by lending it to them, usually against some reserve of coined gold or silver (specie) or perhaps government bonds held by the bank. The populists demanded fair and just access to credit as a basic precondition necessary to enable and sustain broad productive ownership of assets by individuals. The populists identified the policies of private banks as the principal obstacle to providing the credit they needed on the terms they needed it.

Bankers, they argued, whose charters gave them an effective monopoly over credit creation, were able to exploit small businesses and other borrowers of capital, charging them high and unearned rates of interest, and raising and lowering rates to control the money in circulation to their advantage. As a result, populists argued, much of the wealth created by very many borrowers was unjustly appropriated into the hands of a relatively small number of creditors. In the words of a nineteenth-century Arkansas populist, W. Scott Morgan, "Things are neither equal nor equitable, when the holders of money, and evidences of debt which must be liquidated in money, have exclusive power to control and fix the relation between money and commodities which must be parted with to secure money to pay those debts. And this condition does and will exist so long as the holders of this indebtedness have control over the issue of the money, or over any considerable portion of it."[6]

The most radical plan populism produced, and the main theme of this work, is the novel and innovative monetary theory of Edward Kellogg, an antebellum proto-populist writer whose two major works were *Labor and Other Capital: The Rights of Each Secured and the Wrong of Both Eradicated* (1849) and *A New Monetary System: The Only Means of Securing the Respective Rights of Labor and Property and of Protecting the Public from Financial Revulsions* (1861).[7] His was a dramatic and novel proposal to restructure the money system in order to restore economic justice and widely distribute wealth. The idea was to establish a nationally coordinated but decentralized system of locally run public banks. To this end, he developed a unique monetary theory which is the subject of this book, and which remains as relevant as ever in today's crisis-ridden financial world. Populist money would be created by local banks providing loans on a non-profit basis to individuals with good collateral, and in due course extinguished by their repayment, in harmony, they maintained, with the natural cycles of economic life. *The People's Money* aims to update this classical populist monetary vision of public banking for potential application in a modern economy, and to compare it to other current monetary reform proposals, including calls for a return to commodity money (by reestablishing the gold standard), and for the development of a government issued fiat currency (on the model of the Greenbacks).

The tragedy of the populist movement, as we shall see, came with its political defeat in the 1896 election, largely at the hands of the private banking system it opposed, which was able to starve the movement by denying populist cooperatives and other enterprises the credit they needed to succeed. Today, what the populists called unearned or usurious interest rates are presumed as facts of life. The private banking system, though buffeted by recurring crises, has solidified, expanded, and institutionalized its power to the point where it is largely taken for granted. But the issues the populists raised have not gone away. The steady transfer of wealth from borrowers to creditors arguably remains the principal mechanism of economic and social inequality, and by many accounts has intensified in recent decades. Under the circumstances, the monetary reforms proposed by the populists deserve to be revisited.

***

The Peoples' Money is a sequel to two earlier works by the author, *Fixing the System: A History of Populism, Ancient and Modern* (2008), and *The Ecology of Money: Debt, Growth and Sustainability* (2013). The first work, *Fixing the System,* recounted the long history of populist struggles for political and economic democracy. Going back to antiquity, it explored the exploitation of debtors by creditors which has laid at the heart of social inequality ever since. It found populist reformers and revolutionaries to be unique among social critics in placing monetary reform at the center of their agenda. A successor work, *The Ecology of Money*, explored more closely the debtor-creditor relationship. It reexamined the revolution in modern finance begun in the Netherlands and England in the seventeenth and eighteenth centuries. This revolution, ultimately led by private bankers, vastly expanded credit, making the financing of the industrial revolution and modernity itself possible. At the same time it undermined sovereign authority over money creation and ensured that the benefits of the newly created wealth would go disproportionately as unearned income to private creditors charging usurious or exploitative rates of interest.

The Peoples' Money deepens these issues and proposes a remedy. It reviews and updates the innovative monetary solution proposed by nineteenth century American populists in their effort to resolve the inequities of wealth generated by modern finance. Instead of a privatized, for-profit banking system enjoying a state-granted monopoly over the creation of money (the system which has come to dominate Anglo-American and much of Western finance for over the last three centuries), the populists demanded a return to sovereign or state money, to be issued by a decentralized national public banking system under public control. American populists, at their most radical (following Kellogg's ideas), proposed that money be created as loans based on collateral to individuals at local public banks, much as it is created by local branches of private banks in the existing banking system.

Populist public banking, however, would be done on a non-profit basis as a public service. For-profit unearned or usurious interest rates—the engine of economic injustice—would be replaced by a fixed natural rate of interest, at 1%, corresponding, as we shall argue, to the natural rate of resource depreciation over a human lifetime. The populist idea of a fixed natural rate of interest represents an unusual confluence of ecological and monetary thinking which will be explored in this book. From an individual and, by extension, a collective social point of view, the natural 1% rate of interest pegs the rate of creation of money by lending to the need to replace what we consume over time, reflecting a balanced, or steady-state economy.

The populists maintained that political freedom requires the kind of economic security and responsibility that only property ownership is able to provide. By restructuring the monetary system to shift the benefits of credit almost entirely from creditors to borrowers, and by distributing those benefits among many borrowers, the populists aimed to encourage the widespread ownership of property, and thus to promote a democracy of free citizens. With the debt of usurious rates of interest eliminated, borrowers would be freed of the voluntary but practically unavoidable servitude to their creditors which excessive interest rates had required of them. This would allow them to retain, perhaps for the first time in history, the full benefit of their borrowing for themselves and their families.

The father of radical American populist monetary theory was Edward Kellogg (1790–1858), a New York City businessman, author of *Labor and Other Capital* (1849), and the posthumously published *A New Monetary System* (1861). Kellogg influenced subsequent populists, especially Charles Macune, who developed the sub-treasury scheme of the Southern Farmers Alliance designed to provide farmers with credit on the model of Kellogg's system. After the political defeat of the populist movement in 1896, populist monetary theory was largely ignored, and remained of little interest, even among scholars. The recent history of shocks to the private banking system, however, culminating in the crash of 2008 with continued subsequent aftershocks, including the financial stresses of the covid epidemic, have brought issues of debt and monetary reform back to greater public attention. Debt burdens, public and private, have skyrocketed, economic growth has stalled, inflation has grown, and confidence in private banking has been shaken.

The most detailed summary of Kellogg's views and influence remains a nearly century-old essay by Chester McArthur Destler, "The Influence of Edward Kellogg upon American Radicalism, 1865–1896," first published in 1932.[8] Destler credits Kellogg with formulating a series of more or less original propositions about money and the allocation of labor and resources which were variously taken up by radical reformers after the Civil War, including the National Labor Union, the Knights of Labor, the Greenback party, the National Farmers Alliance, and the People's Party.

Destler charts the reprinting of Kellogg's books in the years after the Civil War and his influence upon American radical activists and intellectuals of the time, including Alexander Campbell, William H. Sylvis, William B. Greene, Horace H. Day, Horace Greeley, General S. F. Carey, Britton A. Hill, H. C. Cary, and Charles Macune. These figures, now mostly forgotten, were prominent monetary critics in the ongoing national debates after the Civil War between monetary reformers on the one hand, and private bankers and conservatives on the other, over what the monetary system of the United States ought to be. The war had imposed enormous financial stresses and ballooning debts on both the North and the South, which demanded radical responses. Governments (North and South) went off the gold standard, issued fiat currencies (Greenbacks and Confederate Dollars), sold huge issues of bonds, and, in the North established a new system of a privately owned but nationally regulated system of National Banks. The post war struggle revolved largely around the demand for some form of public money, supported in principle by most radicals, and a restoration of private banking and the gold standard, which became the chief goal of conservatives.[9]

Kellogg's role among the radicals was central but became increasingly diffused over time. Destler presents Kellogg's ideas as somewhat detachable, if potentially consistent, reflecting their varied and often selective appropriation in the political jockeying which marked the political post-war money debate. Destler summarizes the main Kelloggian points as follows: (1) the labor theory of value, (2) the legal tender theory of money, (3) and the interest rate theory of money. The labor theory of value distinguished between productive and non-productive capital, with the former presumed to generate earned income through labor, and the latter unearned income through speculation, which Kellogg compared to gambling. Capital invested in production was presumed to be essential to a healthy functioning economy and society, while capital invested non-productively was condemned as speculation, socially corrosive, and parasitic on someone else's production. The legal tender theory recognized the power of the state to define money in law, in contrast to the private creation of money. And, finally, according to Kellogg's view as Destler puts it, interest was "an all-pervading force, which, by fixing rent and the use of all property, determined the reward of labor."[10] Ultimately, the value of money is the interest rate it can command. Public control over interest rates was perhaps the most fundamental of Kellogg's ideas.

Post–Civil War monetary reformers tended to pick and choose among these options, depending on what they thought would have political appeal at the moment. What they mostly missed (with the particular exception of Charles Macune, who later revived an integrated vision of Kellogg's theory in the programs of the Farmers' Alliance and the People's Party) was the full public banking system presented in *Labor and Other Capital,* and with further detail in *A New Monetary Theory*. Destler's summary of Kellogg's full theory is as follows:

> [T]he plan provided for a paper currency to be issued from a central office with branches in the several states. This currency was to be loaned to individuals, upon real estate security, and at an interest rate uniform throughout the nation. With interest fixed by the government at that rate which would secure to labor and capital their respective rights, and representing actual property in the form of real estate mortgages bearing interest, this currency would possess a uniform value everywhere in the United States. Issued by the central government through the branch loan offices to all who offered good and permanent security, it would free property and labor "from the tyranny . . . exercised over them by the capricious power of money." Finally, to guard against an overissue, and to guarantee to all money the opportunity to accumulate value by interest, this money could be converted at the will of the holders into government bonds, bearing interest

> slightly lower than that charged on mortgage loans. Such a currency . . . would be a perfect and invaluable measure of value. . . . Legal-tender powers would complete its qualifications as a medium of exchange.[11]

It is not altogether clear who may have influenced Kellogg. In an early essay, "A Treatise of the Currency and the Exchanges," he announces, "The conclusions to which I have arrived are somewhat different from what I have seen anywhere else."[12] Destler notes one possible antecedent in Pierre-Joseph Proudhon, whose works circulated in Kellogg's time in New York. In *The Solution of the Social Problem*, Proudhon bemoaned the power of interest on loans to concentrate capital, and the scarcity of gold as the means of final payment limiting available credit. He proposed as a remedy a national bank for France, the Bank of Exchange, which would provide low interest credit by issuing notes to producers on the collateral of their productive assets, in line with Kellogg's later proposal. As he put it, "[T]he problem of the circulation consists in *basing* bank paper, not upon specie, nor bullion, nor immovable property, which can never produce anything but a miserable oscillation between usury and bankruptcy, between the five-franc piece and the assignat; but by basing it upon *products*" (emphasis in original).[13] Whatever the virtues or faults of Proudhon's more inclusive mutualism, or anarchism, his call to make productive assets (farms, shops, mills, factories, mines, stores, lodgings, etc.) instead of precious metals the collateral for public lending became fundamental for Kellogg and subsequently many populists.

The other possible influence on Kellogg Destler suggests was Thomas Mendenhall, also known as Captain Thomas Mendenhall, a seafaring merchant and abolitionist from Wilmington, Delaware (1759–1843), who published a pamphlet on national money in 1816, and a brief *Plan for a National Currency* in 1834.[14] Mendenhall, a critic of the Second National Bank of the United States, and of commodity money in general as a basis for money, called for a paper currency to be backed not by gold or silver but, as Proudhon argued, by the assets of the producing classes. He imagined a National Loan Office to produce the coins and bills, which would then be lent to the states at 4–5% interest, and the states would turn around and lend such money to the general public at 5–6% interest. As long as the public paid interest on their loans, they could retain use of the principle. The interest paid on loans would be deposited in the United States Treasury, which would then return the money so gathered back to the states for improvements and the general welfare.

Kellogg's mature public banking system combined contributions from Proudhon and Mendenhall with his own ideas into a vision of a structured, decentralized, non-profit public banking system where credit is backed by the productive assets of private owners, themselves operating on a capitalistic, for-profit basis. Productive assets are the only real collateral, as they embody the final values of use, and therefore can be the only sufficient backing for a reliable money supply. The evolution of his ideas can be traced to some degree. In his early essay, "Remarks upon Usury and Its Effects: The Evil and a Remedy," a pamphlet he published under the pseudonym 'Whitehook' in 1841,[15] Kellogg mostly railed against the evils of usury, but he also introduced the idea of a new national bank, funded in part by private investors, to provide adequate credit to producers to replace the Second Bank of the United States, extinguished in 1836 after Andrew Jackson's veto. The new national bank would avoid usurious rates by lowering its interest rates and forgoing unearned profits.

In another and apparently subsequent pamphlet, but also anonymously published in 1841, titled *A Treatise on the Currency and the Exchanges*,[16] the national bank disappears in favor of a General Exchange Office, charged with the regulation of a national currency, with private local banks still in control of lending to the public. These early sketches for monetary reform were not yet the full picture of public banking eventually presented in his later, mature book, *Labor and Other Capital* (1849), and in its expanded, posthumously published version in 1861, *A New Monetary System*. In all his works, Kellogg considered labor a unique form of capital: the expenditure of human toil by physical effort, deserving by natural right the fruits of such toil, but deprived of them principally by the monopoly of money creation and allocation held by private bankers, allowing them and their investors to gain unearned income by charging usurious rates of interest.

Kellogg's mature banking system, to be discussed in detail in chapters 3 and 5, is the centerpiece of his monetary theory. Decentralized public banking was his final solution to the evil of concentration of unearned wealth and power, and the subject of this book. After the political defeat of the populists in the 1896 election, his idea of a state sanctioned but decentralized currency issued as credit to borrowers on a non-profit basis as a public service dropped out of sight. The bankers solidified their monetary control behind the shield of the Federal Reserve Bank, created in 1913. Monetary theories came to be seen as quixotic and peripheral. The long twentieth century gave up on trying to replace private money creation with some system of public money creation, and instead narrowed its efforts, at least in the United States, to no more than attempts to regulate the worst excesses of private banking, and then with mixed success. The New Deal banking laws (Federal Deposit Insurance, the Glass-Steagall Act, and others) curbed the most flagrant abuses of private banking for a time, while preserving their effective monopoly over money creation, but these reforms were largely undone by the financial deregulations of the 1980s and 1990s, particularly with the repeal of the Glass-Steagall Act in 1999.

With the increased instability of the American and Western financial systems, however, especially after the global crash of 2008, monetary reform has once more become a pressing issue. The question is what shape it might take. Some reformers today continue to seek a return to commodity money and the gold standard, perhaps including a digital commodity like bitcoin, or perhaps a central bank digital currency (CBDC). Other reformers advocate some kind of fiat money—an unbacked sovereign currency (on the model of the Civil War Greenbacks or the *Assignants* of the French Revolution)—issued solely on the faith and credit of the state. A third alternative—the one advanced in this work—advocates decentralized money creation through lending by many small local public banks, as envisioned by Kellogg and the populists, organized as 'not for profit' public institutions run to provide money to the people as a public service. The money would be provided as credit to be repaid. This was the view of the American populists, yet to be realized in this country. But, as we shall see, important precedents exist elsewhere. A similar system of widespread and successful local banking, the *Sparkassen*, has long been established in Germany, and China, drawing on the German model, dramatically stimulated its economy when it decentralized its state banking system under Deng Xiaoping.

Commodity money and fiat money each pose their own serious problems. Commodity monies historically have proven too scarce and inflexible to provide a basis for the amount of credit needed by complex economies, while fiat currencies have shown themselves vulnerable to inflation and to the inequalities and abuses which come from centralized control. The bankers found a way to expand credit, on the basis of fractional reserve lending, and in doing so they usurped the time-honored power of the sovereign over money creation. The remedy proposed by Kellogg and the populists was to restore public sovereignty over the creation of money, but to continue to create it through the bankers' method of lending on collateral with interest. Populist public banking intended to appropriate and domesticate (not reject) the innovative core lending practices developed by modern private banking, including fractional reserve banking. Kellogg imagined integrating the decentralized creation of bank money (with collateral backing in productive assets) into a system of democratically accountable, sovereign, state banking system to serve public rather than private interests. Public banking on Kellogg's revolutionary model proposes to eliminate the principal scourge of private banking (for-profit, usurious interest rates), while making affordable credit available for individuals willing and able to take on the responsibility of investing in their own future. This work aims to introduce this potentially transformative populist monetary alternative into the current and ever more pressing debate over monetary policy.

NOTES

1. The classic work on American populism remains *The Democratic Promise: The Populist Moment in America*, by Lawrence Goodwyn (New York: Oxford University Press, 1976), abridged as *The Populist Moment: A Short History of the Agrarian Revolt in America* (New York: Oxford University Press, 1978).

See also John D. Hicks, *The Populist Revolt: A History of the Farmers' Alliance and the People's Party* (University of Nebraska, 1961 [1931]; Charles Postel, *The Populist Vision* (New York: Oxford University Press, 2007); Michael Kazin, *The Populist Persuasion: An American History*, revised edition (Ithaca: Cornell University Press, 1995); Robert C. McMath, Jr., *American Populism: A Social History 1877–1898* (New York: Hill and Wang, 1993); Chester McArthur Destler, *American Radicalism: 1865–1901* (Chicago: Quadrangle Books, 1966); Norman Pollack, *The Populist Response to Industrial America: Midwestern Political Thought* (New York: W. W. Norton, 1962). For a general history of populism, see Adrian Kuzminski, *Fixing the System: A History of Populism, Ancient and Modern* (New York: Continuum Books, 2008).

2. Edward Kellogg, *Labor and Other Capital: The Rights of Each Secured and the Wrongs of Both Eradicated* (New York: Augustus M. Kelley, 1971 [1849]), p. xiv.

3. See Norman Pollack, *The Populist Response to Industrial America: Midwestern Populist Thought* (New York: W. W. Norton, 1962), chapters 2 and 3.

4. Even today small businesses (less than five hundred employees) constitute over 99 percent of all business, half of private sector workforce, most new jobs, and over 40 percent of the economy: "State of Small Business Now" (US Chamber of Commerce, April 2023), https://www.uschamber.com/small-business/state-of-small-business-now.

5. Tocqueville, Alexis de, *Democracy in America*. Henry Reeve, trans. Vols. I and II (New York: Bantam Books, 2002); for a good snapshot of the Jeffersonian world, see Dominick J. Reisen, *Middlefield and the Settling of the New York Frontier* (Voorheesville: Square Circle Press, 2009).

6. W. Scott Mogan, "Overproduction—the Law of Supply and Demand," in *A Populist Reader: Selections from the Works of American Populist Leaders*, George Brown Tindall, ed. (New York: Harper & Row, 1966), p. 13.

7. Edward Kellogg, *Labor and Other Capital: The Rights of Each Secured and the Wrongs of Both Eradicated* (New York: Augustus Kelley, 1971 [1849]); and *A New Monetary System: The Only Means of Securing the Respective Rights of Labor and Property and of Protecting the Public from Financial Revulsions* (New York: Burt Franklin, 1970 [1861]).

8. Chester McArthur Destler, "The Influence of Edward Kellogg upon American Radicalism, 1865-1896," *Journal of Political Economy* XL (June 1932), pp. 338–65; reprinted in Chester McArthur Destler, *American Radicalism 1865–1901* (New London: Connecticut College, 1946), pp. 50–77.

9. A recent account of Civil War and post–Civil War monetary and financial policies and debates can be found in Roger Lowenstein, *Ways and Means: Lincoln and*

His Cabinet and the Financing of the Civil War (New York: Penguin, 2023), et. passim.

10. Destler, op.cit., p. 53.

11. Ibid., pp. 54–55

12. Edward Kellogg [Unknown Author], *A Treatise on the Currency and the Exchanges: Proposing a Remedy for the Evil That Exist in Relation to Them, by the Establishment of a General Exchange Office, Which Shall Also Be the Fiscal Agent of Government* (New York: Hopkins and Jennings, September, 1841), p. 3, https://books.google.je/books?id=4jgKAQAAMAAJ&printsec=frontcover#v=onepage&q&f=false.

13. Pierre-Joseph Proudhoun, *The Solution of the Social Problem* [Excerpts] (The Anarchist Library, 2012), Part IV, "The Bank of Exchange," https://theanarchistlibrary.org/library/pierre-joseph-proudhon-the-solution-of-the-social-problem.

14. Thomas Mendenhall, *A New Plan for a National Currency* (Philadelphia: J Rakestraw, 1834) https://archive.org/details/newplanfornation0000thom&view=theater.

15. See Edward Kellogg {Whitehook], "Remarks upon Usury and its Effects: A National Bank a Remedy" (New York: Harper and Brothers, 1841) https://www.libertarian-labyrinth.org/from-the-archives/edward-kellogg-remarks-upon-usury/.

16. See Edward Kellogg [Unknown Author], *A Treatise on the Currency and the Exchanges: Proposing a Remedy for the Evil That Exist in Relation to Them, by the Establishment of a General Exchange Office, Which Shall Also Be the Fiscal Agent of Government* (New York: Hopkins and Jennings, September, 1841), https://books.google.je/books?id=4jgKAQAAMAAJ&printsec=frontcover#v=onepage&q&f=false.

Chapter 1

The Bankers' Monopoly

The major cause of the deep inequalities of wealth found in our society is a simple mechanism which keeps it all going: the state-chartered monopoly power held by private banks to create money by issuing loans simply entered as deposits in their borrowers' accounts, and to profit from the interest charged on those loans. Their lending is limited only by the pool of borrowers, and the need to keep enough assets in reserve to cover any withdrawals made by deposit holders. When bankers first discovered (over three hundred years ago) that they could lend out more money than they had on hand, they still had to be careful to maintain minimum cash reserves to accommodate withdrawals. These reserves (at first coins held in bank vaults, and later government bonds and legal tender bills) eventually evolved into the complex capital security holdings required by modern banks, ultimately regulated under a series of international agreements called the Basel Accords (coordinated through the Bank for International Settlements (BIS) in Basel, Switzerland, beginning in 1988.)[1]

The principle, however, has remained the same all along: banks continue to enjoy the ability to create far more new money through lending than their relatively small base of assets would seem to indicate. This publicly sanctioned, privatized, for-profit, credit-based monetary system in effect transforms the wealth earned by the labor of debtors (who have to work to pay back principal and interest) into unearned wealth held by creditors. Banks have not earned the money they lend out as deposits; they do not even possess it before they lend it. Instead they create it, literally out of nothing, in the very act of lending it out. They do so by a bookkeeping entry, by simply crediting the deposit accounts of borrowers for the amounts they agree to lend to them, albeit with the backing of the borrowers' collateral or other equivalent assurances. The borrower agrees to repay the loan over time with interest. The creation of money takes place through a formal loan agreement, or contract, a binding matter of legal record. Nearly all money in modern capitalistic economies, especially in Western countries, is created in this way.[2]

Money creation through bank lending was perhaps more evident to people in an earlier time when many small producers (the bulk of the population) relied on local bank loans to finance their businesses. With the growth and consolidation of banking in the nineteenth century, however, alternate explanations of banking were widely offered, in part to ward off critics. In his essay "A Lost Century of Economics,"[3] monetary theorist Richard Werner sums up the major schools of banking theory as follows:

> during different time periods of the 20th century, one of three distinct and mutually exclusive theories of banking has been dominant: The oldest, the *credit creation theory of banking*, maintains that each bank can individually create money "out of nothing" through accounting operations, and does so when extending a loan. The *fractional reserve theory* states that only the banking system as a whole can collectively create money, while each individual bank is a mere financial intermediary, gathering deposits and lending these out. The *financial intermediation theory* considers banks as financial intermediaries both individually and collectively, rendering them indistinguishable from other non-bank financial institutions in their behaviour, especially concerning the deposit and lending businesses, being unable to create money individually or collectively. (Emphasis in original)[4]

Werner's first theory—the credit creation theory—dovetails nicely with the populist view of bank money to be explored in this work, where money is created as loans on collateral with interest. Werner traces the credit creation theory back not, as we will, to its earliest manifestations among seventeenth century London goldsmiths, but to Henry D. Macleod's two-volume 1856 work, *The Theory and Practice of Banking*. According to Macleod, as quoted by Werner,

> Bankers, no doubt, do collect sums from a vast number of persons, but the peculiar essence of their business is, not to lend that money to other persons, but on the basis of this bullion to create a vast superstructure of Credit; to multiply their promises to pay many times: these Credits being payable on demand and performing all the functions of an equal amount of cash. Thus banking is not an Economy of Capital, but an increase of Capital; *the business of banking is not to lend money, but to create Credit*: and by means of the Clearing House these Credits are now transferred from one bank to another, just as easily as a Credit is transferred from one account to another in the same bank by means of a cheque. And all these Credits are in the ordinary language and practice of commerce exactly equal to so much cash or Currency. (Emphasis in original)[5]

The amount of deposits in a bank, or the extent of its private capital, is distinguished in credit creation theory from the bank's separate ability to create money by crediting depositor's accounts. If it doesn't come from its deposits, where does a bank get the money with which it credits a borrower's account? Werner answers as follows:

> The money was not withdrawn by the bank from other uses. It was not diverted or transferred from any other part of the economy. Most of all, although it is shown as a deposit, it was not actually deposited by anyone. The bank simply created the money by writing the figures into its books and the customer's account book. In effect, the bank pretends that its borrower has made a deposit that was not actually made. Unlike the textbook representation, we see that each individual bank can thus create money when it extends a loan. *Showing this truth in textbooks would not only be more memorable, but it would also teach students about what banks really do: they create money out of nothing. The bank just pretends it has the* [*loan amounts*], *credits someone's books with them, and nobody knows the difference.*[6]Thus banking is not an Economy of Capital, but an increase of Capital; *the business of banking is not to lend money, but to create Credit*: and by means of the Clearing House these Credits are now transferred from one bank to another, just as easily as a Credit is transferred from one account to another in the same bank by means of a cheque. (Emphasis in original)

Werner's two other theories of banking both represent banks as financial intermediaries, where banks 'just collect deposits and lend them out.' Werner traces the intermediation theory back to Ludwig von Mises's 1912 book, *The Theory of Money and Credit*, where von Mises writes,"Only those who lend the money of others are bankers; those who merely lend their own capital are capitalists, but not bankers."[7] The idea is that, since bankers supposedly only lend money already placed on account by depositors, their function is to bring together, or intermediate, between savers and borrowers. Support can be found in John Maynard Keynes's *General Theory* that savings must proceed investment, and among many other economists Werner cites. The very simplicity of the intermediation theory, he points out, excludes bankers from any closer scrutiny. If they are merely lending out the savings their depositors have already put in account, banking appears a fully transparent process, and hardly different from any other lending, and with no particular reason to be regulated. The role of money in economic life becomes invisible.

Werner describes fractional reserve banking as a form of intermediation. This, however, muddies the waters. To see why, some background on fractional reserve banking may be useful. Traditional fractional reserve banking seems to have been conceived, as we shall see, by the seventeenth century goldsmiths of London, and then institutionalized by the Bank of England, and later epitomized in the United States by the 'free banking' era between Andrew Jackon's final overthrow of the Second National Bank in 1836 and the Civil War. States in that era chartered private banks, but reserve requirements were variable and loose, and banks often tended to issue loans in excess of their reserves. This was feasible for them because depositors of gold and silver were given bank notes, paper bills or certificates, which circulated among the public as the currency of general exchange and were accepted as a substitute for cash at par, forestalling immediate withdrawals from the bank. In the meantime, bankers kept ahead of withdrawals by steadily collecting repayments of principal, along with interest.

Fractional reserve banking—as pioneered by the London goldsmiths in the seventeenth century—works insofar as the bank's certificates representing hard cash, or specie, come to function as money in place of hard cash, or specie. The principle behind traditional fractional reserve banking (excess lending on reserves) was already apparent with John Law's French national bank between 1716 and 1720 (the *Banque Générale Privée*). The spectacular failure of his bank, along with the associated Mississippi Company, gave fractional reserve banking a bad name. In the decades which followed, bankers, who continued to employ the principle of fractional reserve lending, even in Britain, had to evade or bear the suspicion which often accompanied the practice. Unwilling to abandon the profits generated by fractional reserve lending, bankers came up with a face-saving rationale pitched to portray the innocence of the practice. To avoid calling attention to something difficult to explain, and counterintuitive, but central to their business model, bankers promoted ingenious reassurances that fractional reserve banking is not what it appears to be, that the money being lent out really does come from deposits, and is not invented, and that banks only intermediate between depositors and borrowers.

It is important to be clear that banks no longer practice fractional reserve banking in its original or narrow sense. Banks today are no longer isolated stand-alone businesses required to keep a minimum of cash literally on hand to redeem bank notes which they themselves have printed and issued to depositors as loans. Today almost every bank is an integral part of a network of banks which enjoys the backup of a central bank. It is the system as a whole, coordinated by a central bank, which stands as an aggregate of reserves in place of the cash in the vault of any individual bank. Cash in the vault as a reserve has been replaced by capital requirements managed by the Federal Reserve and government officials to regulate the system.[8] Deposit insurance and government guarantees further insulate banks against excess demands by depositors to get cash for their money on account. Individual bank runs continue to occur, but they have been contained within the larger system since the Great Depression. Fractional reserve banking, however, has quietly continued to beat at the heart of the private banking system. It has been institutionalized on a system-wide basis. Its risks have not been eliminated but universalized. Future failure is likely to be systemically catastrophic rather than locally disruptive.

It has remained in the interest of bankers to disguise the fractional reserve principle on which they continue to operate for their private profit. While one bank might appear to be lending more than it should, the banker's defense has been that deposits even out over the system as a whole. How might this deception work? Friedrich von Hayek, Werner tells us, "argued that with a reserve of 10%, every bank would lend out 90% of any deposit, which would increase deposits with other banks, resulting in a multiple creation of deposits in the banking system."[9] The process begins when depositors deposit their savings in Bank A. That bank, in Hayek's example, then lends out 90% of its deposits, keeping 10% in reserve, to other borrowers. These borrowed funds in turn are spent on goods and services. The sellers of those goods and services receive and deposit this money as their 'savings' in Bank B, which in turn lends out 90% of the original 90%, which then ends up in Bank C, and so on until the cumulative 90% iterations of the original loan were exhausted. The idea was to deny that banks create money 'out of nothing' by fractional reserve banking, but rather that the same old money is somehow transferred from bank to bank in the course of normal financial transactions. This is the argument for systematic intermediation between the banks as a whole and the public.

This theory of intermediation, as Werner points out, was enshrined in Paul Samuelson's famous textbook, *Economics* (1948, and in many subsequent editions). In Samuelson's version of the model the money lent by each bank is presumed to have been deposited in the bank, not created out of nothing. In relending 90% of its savings deposits, Bank A is said to perform its intermediation function matching savers with borrowers, as do Banks B and C in turn, as described above. The increase in money, it is argued, comes entirely from the multiplier effect of gradually decreasing amounts lent out over and over in the system, not by the actions of any one bank. A single bank may appear to operate on a fractional reserve basis, but this is only because the system as a whole functions on a full reserve basis whether or not individual banks do. The effect of this argument is to portray fractional reserve banking as a natural function of intermediation by the banking system as a whole. Money is not created out of nothing, we are reassured, but consists entirely of deposits being lent and re-lent, ultimately redeemable in units of final payment, or cash, traditionally specie (coined precious metals) or, today, federal reserve notes. The cash basis of money does not change, it is claimed, but is simply multiplied through reuse.

Werner went so far as to attempt to demonstrate the fictitiousness of the intermediary and disguised fractional reserve theories by an empirical test. In a 2014 paper, "Can Banks Individually Create Money Out of Nothing?"

Werner reports on his experiment to conduct an "empirical test" as money is "borrowed from a cooperating bank, while its internal records are being monitored, to establish whether in the process of making the loan available to the borrower, the bank transfers these funds from other accounts within or outside the bank, or whether they are newly created. This study establishes for the first time empirically that banks individually create money out of nothing."[10] The recorded step-by-step analysis of a loan transaction by a German cooperative bank failed to disclose, at any point in making the loan available to the borrower, that the bank transferred any funds from other accounts within or outside the bank to complete the process. Instead, the loan funds were simply entered by the bank in the account of the borrower. Werner shows that the money supply can be augmented by a single loan by a single bank, without requiring the repeated relending of a decreasing portion of the original loan throughout the banking system.

Werner's experiment demonstrates not only that money can be created out of nothing, but that in our system it actually occurs when bankers make loans through the credit creation theory on a fractional reserve basis. The government creates money when it mints coins and prints dollars, it is true, but the vast bulk of money is created through bank loans, and these are multiplied many times over by the bank's reliance on reserves which are only a fraction of what it lends out. The notion of a simple creation of money can be misleading. Banks cannot create money as they please if they want to stay in business. They do so not only on a reserve basis, but also on the condition that there are willing borrowers available with a reasonable prospect of repayment of principal and interest. This essential background is often overlooked or taken for granted. Without this condition, the banking business model collapses. The collateral of the borrowers provides the ultimate backing for the money the bankers create. By collapsing fractional reserve banking into intermediation, Werner obscures the issue, and allows the hidden power of reserve banking to continue to escape public attention.

Banking continues to provide intermediation, to be sure, only it is between the credit creation they are licensed to offer through their charters, and the needs of their borrowers, not between savings and lending. Banking continues to rely on fractional reserve lending, insofar as the money of account banks create as credit significantly exceeds the actual cash available at any time (physical coins and Federal Reserve Notes). Bank money, or credit, is money of account. It circulates on the presumption that it can be redeemed in cash, even if it never is. Bank money, or money of account, is technically not a means of final payment, as cash is, but only a promise to provide final payment if it is demanded. Normally, however, bank money is accepted as if it were the final payment. But if bank money is questioned, and confidence in its soundness is lost, then final payment, or cash, will be demanded (as in a bank run).

What Werner has shown by his experiment is that there is a kind of money we can call credit money, or bank money, and that it has become the normal form of money, or currency, for most transactions in Western countries. Banking itself stands revealed as money creation by credit issued on collateral with conditions of repayment, even if this is seldom publicly admitted. This stands in contrast with two other forms of money Werner does not discuss: commodity money and fiat money. Commodity money (generally gold or silver) formed the cash (final payment) basis of traditional bank money, as noted above, while fiat money (coin, paper, or digital) relies on the authority of the government, including its monopoly over force and taxation, to guarantee its value. Fiat money cannot be redeemed except with more fiat money. In what follows, we will explore some of the shortcomings of both commodity and fiat monies, and the contrasting advantages of bank money (Werner's 'credit creation' theory of money) as a form of money. We will also argue that banking is a natural monopoly, and therefore should be run as a public, nonprofit enterprise, and not as a for-profit private business. This tension between the private interest of the bankers in maintaining their control over money creation, and the conflicting presumption of the public that the creation of money ought to be the duty of the sovereign, as it had been under traditional sovereigns (monarchies, republics, democracies), has been an important fault line in the controversies over money and banking.

***

The deeper struggle between public and private interests over the control of money and banking found its classic expression in the debate between the so-called Currency and Banking schools in nineteenth century Britain.[11] In the eighteenth and early nineteenth centuries, the money supply in Britain was dramatically expanded by private banks creating money by lending on a fractional reserve basis. Individual banks would issue their own notes, on the basis of their own reserves, with little or no regulation. The banking school applauded this freedom, and argued that market competition in banking, or 'free banking,' would naturally regulate interest rates and the supply of money lent out. However, too many banks continued to make too many bad loans, leading to periodic panics and bankruptcies and calls for banking reform.

To gain control over the wildly fluctuating money supply, reformers of the so-called Currency school, led by David Ricardo, urged the British government to intervene. It did so, culminating in the Bank Charter Act of 1844, which allowed only the notes of the Bank of England to circulate as cash—legal tender or physical money of final payment—and only to the extent of

100% backing in gold reserves. The bank's issuance department was separated from its lending department; the latter, however, along with those of other banks, could still issue loans as money of account on deposit. Money of account created as loan credit evaded the constraints of limited cash and continued to swell banking speculation and fuel further crises and panics.

The Currency vs. Banking debate set the terms for the subsequent debate between private and public interests over control over money creation, especially in English-speaking countries. As bankers continued to promote their privileged monopoly, the Currency school insisted more and more on some form of state money creation as an alternative to unstable bankers' money. Joseph Huber draws the conclusion that

> currency-school teachings established as a matter of experience and empirical fact that modern money is fiat money which can freely be created. In the absence of proper regulation, free creation of bank money (banknotes, demand deposits) tends to procyclically overshoot, then temporarily shrink, and be in final consequence without restraint. It results in an unstable and ultimately inflationary and asset inflationary money supply which induces financial and economic crises. Therefore, from a currency point of view it needs to be determined by law what shall be money in the sense of currency in general circulation, under whose control and responsibility modern fiat money shall be created, according to what procedures, and who shall benefit from the seigniorage, i.e., the special profit that accrues from creating new currency.[12]

Currency school reformers still had to face the question of the proper backing for any government issued fiat currency. Even the popular gold standard of the nineteenth century had to be periodically suspended due to wars, revolutions, disruptions, and depressions. Subsequent proposals for monetary backing (a basket of currencies and/or commodities, or GNP, or the simple taxation power of government) have proved no more reliable. The long-term failure of the Currency school to establish a convincing theory, or set of rules, for state management of fiat currency has given the Banking school room to push back. Bankers offered in response the 'real bills' doctrine, so-called from the bankers' claim that money lent on good credit (originally on the reliable notes, or 'real bills' of reputable firms) is the money most likely to be repaid. The repayment of debt, the bankers argued, is the principal instrument for the extinction of money, which is necessary to counter its inflationary creation.

At stake here was the legitimacy of fractional reserve banking. The Currency school in the end rejects the idea; the Banking school endorses it. Fractional reserve lending, as we shall see in more detail, was the invention of private bankers, who used it to usurp what had been the money creation monopoly of the state, or the sovereign. Currency school reformers have aimed to reestablish sovereign control over money creation, but with no intention of preserving fractional reserve banking, and even hostility towards it. The well-known Chicago Plan of the 1930s, developed by University of Chicago economists (led by Henry Simons), along with Irving Fisher, reflects the reformers' long war against fractional reserve banking.[13] It proposed, following Ricardo, to separate the issuing from the lending of money. The government would issue a new fiat currency as an instrument of legal tender and final payment, and fractional reserve banking would be effectively outlawed. Banks would no longer create money through fractional reserve lending but would be able to lend solely on their private equity of accumulated fiat money for funds to lend out. They could no longer mix their deposit accounts with their lending accounts; deposits would have to be backed 100% by reserves in the new currency.

The Chicago Plan has remained the template for fiat money reformers. Its "Achilles heel," as Charles Goodhart and Meinhard Jensen put it,[14] is its inability to distinguish between real money and near or representative money. No matter what the fiat currency may be, other alternate forms of contractual promises of future payment, which can effectively function in place of real money, or cash, will continue to be invented by clever investors, a process already evident in the shadow banking system. Fractional reserve banking seems likely to continue to appear in new forms, even if chartered banks are not allowed to practice it.

A larger issue for Currency school reformers is the very nature of the fiat money they propose. If it is to be issued into existence 'out of nothing' not by bankers' loans but by state fiat, to pay its expenses on a continuing basis (to fund bureaucracies, the military, government contractors, social services, entitlements, etc.), government money will circulate into the economy up to the amount of cash it spends. Arguably, the best precedent for this remains the greenback fiat money experiment of the United States government for a period during and after the Civil War. Whatever the nature of the currency (coins, paper notes, digital entries, etc.), the idea is for the government to spend it directly into circulation. To avoid perpetual inflation, some method for the government to extinguish the money it has created is necessary. The principal tool for this is taxation, but taxation would have to equal spending over time in order to stabilize the money supply—a self-defeating goal. Moreover, and not least, the money creation which is currently dispersed and decentralized in the United States in thousands of banks and other lending institutions would be concentrated solely in the hands of the federal government. Money creation, which is now a matter of millions of separate private loan contracts with thousands of banks, would be centralized in the federal budget, and subject to deliberate political direction. A strong form of state economic planning would appear to be a likely result.

The novelty of American populist theory of money creation through public banking is highlighted when understood in terms of the long running debate between the Currency and Banking schools. Unlike the Banking tradition, which represents the interests of private bank money creation, populist public banking is public, and intended in the public interest. It agrees with the Currency tradition in seeking to restore the money power to the sovereign. Unlike the Currency tradition, however, the populist tradition retains fractional reserve banking as the principal mechanism of money creation, only shifting it from private to public. It rejects the idea of fiat money and argues instead that the creation of money 'out of nothing' through lending remains the best mechanism for a stable money supply. The Currency tradition has to provide a convincing alternative to the Bankers method of balancing money creation and extinction through loan creation and repayment.

Populist money-creating banking would retain the private bankers mechanism of money creation through lending and turn it into a public service, run at cost, not for profit, leaving borrowers full benefit of their loans. The populists also agree with the bankers, on the other hand, that money creation through personal loan contracts be made available directly and exclusively to the people locally throughout the country, and not concentrated in a few hands at the federal level, as the Currency tradition has traditionally presumed. Money would be issued to the public locally, and percolate up through the economy, instead of being issued nationally, and then circulating down into the economy through the hands of government contractors and dependents.

***

This astonishing creation of money out of nothing by the banks is an open secret among bankers, financiers, analysts, scholars, and interested parties, but it remains largely unknown to the general public. If asked how money is created, a typical person might likely say that money, at least in the United States, is created not by regular banks, but by the government, or perhaps more precisely, by the Federal Reserve, understood to be a government agency. They might add, if they've taken an economics course, that while the Treasury Department prints paper bills and mints metal coins at the request of the Fed, these are but a miniscule percentage of the money in circulation. Most money, they might go on to say, is created when the Fed puts dollars into circulation by buying government bonds from the private banks who bought them from the government in the first place, originally out of their own savings from commercial lending. Selling government bonds to the Fed leaves the private banks with more money on account, which allows them to lend more to the public, thus stimulating the economy.

This process, we are told, works in reverse as well when the central bank sells government bonds for dollars, taking them out of circulation and dampening the economy. The picture we are invited to imagine is that of a top-down banking system, with a central bank (the Fed, or the European Central Bank, or any other central bank) creating money by buying government debt from private banks, and extinguishing it by selling government debt back to the same private banks. The Fed, in this view, has its hand on the money spigot, and opens and closes it to control the flow of money down through the commercial banks and into the everyday economy.

This is a partial but very misleading picture, which obscures far more than it reveals. The function of the Fed is not to create the money itself, but to protect and regulate the money creation that is actually carried out by private bank lending. It functions as a bank for bankers, not for the public. Private banks hold accounts at the Fed, much as the public holds accounts at private banks. Bank accounts at the Fed provide a record of their solvency, much as do accounts held at private banks by the public. In both cases, the point is not to overdraw one's account. By raising and lowering short-term interest rates, the Fed raises and lowers the reserves or capital, or other equivalent collateral private banks must secure with the Fed to remain solvent. The ability to raise or lower rates using the Federal Funds rate also lowers and raises the supply of money, which in turn affects the economy. The Fed's ability to adjust rates rationalizes and stabilizes the financial system to the benefit of the bankers. The Fed, with minimal and wholly inadequate public accountability, operates largely through the Federal Reserve Bank of New York. It primarily serves the interest of the Manhattan banks, that are 100% owners of the Federal Reserve Bank of New York, and only secondarily those of thousands of local banks, or the general public. The purpose of a central bank like the Fed is to secure the collective security of a cartel (the New York City big bank network) and help it maintain its for-profit monopoly over the money system.

The Fed does not create most of the money in circulation, and never has. That has been done all along by private banks. We have never had a top-down banking system in the United States as is widely presumed. A central bank, like the Fed, is a bank only for banks; its members (and also owners, in the case of the New York Fed) are the private commercial banks which dominate the industry. They, along with the federal government (plus the Treasury Department and a few other federal agencies), alone have accounts at the Fed. Just as commercial banks lend by creating deposits (money) in their customers' accounts, so the central bank lends by creating deposits (money) in the accounts of commercial banks, as well as in the accounts of the federal government held at the Fed. Both the central bank and the commercial banks enjoy the power of money creation, it is true, but central bank money creation is highly restricted; it is available only to commercial banks who have accounts with, and are members of, the central bank, or the government. Central bank money creation is conspicuously not available to the public, who do not have accounts with the Fed. Instead we must use the money created for us by loans from commercial banks, where we can have accounts.

In sum, in practice there are two kinds of money, or more accurately, two separate systems of the same kind of money: closed central bank money denominated in dollars and held on account by member banks exclusively at the Fed, and open commercial bank money denominated in dollars and held on account by the public only at banks and related institutions (such as savings and loans, thrifts, and credit unions, all regulated to receive deposits under banking rules). The money created by commercial banks is the public money we all use (along with the coins and printed bills of the Treasury). In contrast to the picture of the Fed as the ultimate creator of money, most money, it turns out, is created by thousands of private banks making millions of loans to individuals and businesses all across the country.

To stay in business, member banks must maintain such reserves, or their equivalent, as required to clear their accounts at the central bank. This is the very definition of solvency. The central bank creates money just as the commercial banks do: by 'selling' the money they create in return for 'buying' debt of the borrower. The central bank 'buys' the debt of the commercial banks, just as the commercial banks 'buy' the debt of the public. The central bank credits the accounts of commercial banks (internal money creation) in return for receiving their bonds and other securities, just as commercial banks credit the accounts of the public (external money creation) in return for receiving their debts (mortgages, credit cards, etc.).

The two kinds of money do not mix. The accounts remain on two different levels. Member banks may use their accounts at the central bank to settle transactions among themselves, and to lend and borrow from one another, and from the central bank. But it is the money they create by lending to the public, which is their original and main business; their common membership in a central bank provides for them an association or organization where otherwise independent member banks are able to cooperate together as a cartel to coordinate and facilitate their collective interests. In the crisis of the 1930s, the Fed allowed thousands of non-member banks to go bankrupt, setting a pattern for consolidation through big banks swallowing smaller, struggling competitors.

The debt-created dual system of bank money just described is entirely money of account. It is represented by certain physical objects (numbers on computer screens, signatures on checks, printed bank statements, invoices, etc.), but it does not itself physically exist. It exists only mentally, in the imagination, as an obligation to be redeemed in the future. A unit of bank money, a dollar or a pound, is a ticket good for some future consumption; it is a claim against some measure of the goods and services for sale on the market. There is only one other kind of money besides bank money, which we can call hard or physical money, or cash. Cash is the last token, or final payment; it is the last thing which can be demanded to complete a transaction. Unlike money of account, it exists not only in the imagination, but crucially in reality as well. Historically, many tangible objects have served as commodity monies, or cash (wampum, beads, beaver pelts, jewelry, salt, grain, paper, iron, copper, silver, and gold, among many others, including bills, or paper notes), but convenience and custom have gradually settled on precious metals, usually gold and silver, and suitably engraved paper notes, or bills. Today in the United States, commodity monies or cash take two forms: minted Treasury coins and printed Federal Reserve notes.

Nearly all of our money, however, is bank money, or money of account, not cash. Under normal circumstances, the transfer of funds by debiting one account and crediting another is usually sufficient to stand as final payment to close a transaction. Very few people today buy a house, or a car, or appliances, or clothes, or even groceries or a restaurant meal, with cash. Most commonly, credit or debit cards or a phone app are swiped, and accounts are appropriately debited and credited by the computers of the banking system. Little if any cash is needed for most transactions. It is only in the event of a financial crash, when the credit system of the banks collapses, that credit is no longer sufficient as final payment, and that cash is suddenly in demand.

The classic example is a bank run, as in the film *It's a Wonderful Life*, where depositors suddenly demand their money back over the counter, in actual dollars, or printed currency. Today, they would not demand cash from frightened bank tellers; they would demand transfer of balances from their accounts to other, safer accounts, in other, safer banks, which can be done electronically in a split second. But if the safety of further banks comes into question, depositors will ultimately demand cash from them as well, as in the movie. Cash is ultimately physical money, something which anyone can carry in their pocket. In a deep enough crisis, substitutes for cash will no longer be accepted. In the end, thoroughly panicked depositors will want money as a tangible, physical token, such as actual Federal Reserve Notes, or coins, as the means for final payment.

Having a central bank provides member banks a cushion against crashes and bank runs. Nonetheless, if a bank cannot maintain its reserves at the Fed, it is bankrupt, just as a business that cannot maintain its reserves with its commercial bank is bankrupt. Unless, that is, it is 'too big to fail.' Unlike commercial banks, which do not bail out their borrowers, the central bank is usually prepared to bail out its borrowers—its member banks—if necessary. The central bank stands as a lender of last resort behind its member banks, ready to create central bank money to lend to them as needed. As part of its role as a backstop, the central bank provides the services which enable exchanges among commercial banks to continue. By keeping reserve accounts at a central bank and being part of its network, commercial banks are able to transfer funds through withdrawals and deposits on one another's accounts, and to reconcile discrepancies by borrowing from one another or from the Fed itself. Individual Federal Reserve Banks distribute currency and coins to member banks, lend money to them, and process their electronic payments.

A central bank like the Federal Reserve is effectively a mutual aid society which the large New York banks have set up for themselves, largely in self-defense against their critics. A central bank makes it possible for bankers to rationalize their own industry. It provides a coordinating mechanism essential to advancing the members' collective interests. After the panic of 1907, in the face of public uproar and Congressional inquiries, leading American bankers, led by J. P. Morgan, agreed to cooperate together with Congress in support of banking reform they said would prevent future financial crises and panics. They convinced Congress to establish a state-sponsored central bank, the Fed, which was accomplished through the Federal Reserve Act of 1913. The act gave the private banking system a cover of public legitimacy without changing its fundamental nature as a private for-profit monopoly enterprise. The Fed was, and remains, a private–public hybrid in which those who were supposedly regulated (the bankers, particularly the owners of the New York Fed) from the very beginning captured the power of the supposed regulators (the federal government) for their own protection and benefit.

The central bank—the Fed—has no direct access to the public. Its officials are appointed for lengthy terms, come mostly from the banking world, and are minimally accountable to the public. The money the Fed creates does not directly get into the larger economy, as we have seen. It is the private banks (and the related depository institutions under their wing, like credit unions and savings and loans) who enjoy the monopoly of creating money for the public and the larger economy as a whole, with the backing of the central bank, which they own. The Fed is the tail which does not wag the dog. The bankers private monopoly is protected and strengthened by the central bank bulwark they have inserted between themselves and the public, even as banks compete among themselves to grow or be swallowed by still larger banks. The banking cartel is a club whose members hold charters allowing them the power to create money by lending, and to profit from it. The populists understood it as a license to steal. It is commercial banks, the largest ones, who control the industry, not the central bank, which is their shield.[15]

As a result, the private bankers have been able to safely exercise their monopolistic right to accommodate debt-seeking customers from the general public (at least those who have adequate collateral) by creating as loans to them (that is, to us as borrowers) the debt-money which is the only money we can use. Best of all for the banks, the whole scheme has the imprimatur of the state, that is, of the sovereign (via the 1913 Federal Reserve Act and subsequent legislation). The banking system can thereby claim a kind of popular legitimacy. The Fed in return takes the heat from banking critics and protects the private banking monopoly from any serious public oversight.

It's a perfect smokescreen. The public thinks the Fed regulates the banks, whereas the banks regulate the Fed, or, to be more accurate, the big banks regulate the Fed while dominating the small banks under their umbrella. Keeping a reserve account at the Fed is a cheap price for commercial banks to pay for insuring and disciplining their money-making monopoly. The Federal Reserve Act of 1913 reserved the subcontracting of the creation of money to the public as the virtually exclusive domain of private banks, which need to be granted a charter to join the club and play the game. Yet there is nothing about money creation—no special property, or resource, or skill—which suggests it ought to be a privilege reserved for private, for-profit, monopolistic bankers and their descendants—even if they invented it.[16]

The monopoly power to create money allows commercial banks to charge the public a discretionary fee (a variable rate of interest) for the privilege of borrowing the money they create for them. It further allows them the private use of most of that money as long as it remains on deposit with them. The amount of money on deposit (plus their assets) allows banks to lend on a fractional reserve basis, multiplying credit and their private profit. The Fed officially sets interest rates by setting the Federal Funds Rate for member banks borrowing and lending central bank money. But causation actually runs the other way. The Fed's Funds Rate largely reflects the demands and needs of member banks, and only secondarily what the Fed may think its members need. Raising or lowering the rate in the face of member bank resistance is possible only to the extent to which the dominant private banks go along for their own good, or for their own survival. Monopoly power also gives the larger banks, in the event of liquidation of weaker banks, the opportunity to profit by consolidation of the industry, and to absorb lesser players in the process. The Fed modulates and dampens this process of boom and bust for the benefit of the member banks, especially the dominant banks. Without the Fed, there would be a chaotic free-for-all reminiscent of the 'wild cat' banking familiar in the United States in the early nineteenth century. With the Fed in place, however, private banks have the benefits of mutual cooperation and a bailout protection plan behind a facade of government regulation.

The ability of banks to create and manipulate interest rates on debt lies at the heart of their system; it is the major mechanism producing their profits. Their ability to lend out most of the borrowers' money on deposit on a fractional reserve basis for their own investment compounds their monopoly power. The privatized banking system, relying on the Fed to set and vary interest rates in its loans to the public, has the ability to adjust the value of money to maximize its returns or minimize its losses. The rate of interest is otherwise limited only by a reliable demand for loans, that is, by willing and able borrowers. Recurrent bank crises were common in the decades up to the Depression, but New Deal reforms (including Federal Deposit Insurance Corporation established to protect depositors) stabilized the system. The Glass-Steagall Act of 1933, separating commercial from investment banking, also provided an important check on banking excesses, until it was repealed in 1999. Thanks to these reforms, the system functioned reasonably well to the bankers benefit between the Depression and the crash of 2008, when it was overwhelmed by the unregulated growth and sudden collapse of the so-called 'shadow banking' system.

There is one more major player who has lately emerged in the money credit creation game. Unlike regular chartered banks, shadow banks (finance companies, hedge funds, insurance companies, money market mutual funds, and other private pools of money) do not create money by crediting the deposit accounts of customers (or lending it into existence) as banks do; rather they are non-bank financial institutions which add value, generally by repackaging various debt instruments derived from original bank lending and recirculating them among investors. Operating under far fewer regulations than regular banks, shadow banks piggy-back on normal bank operations. They amplify returns for investors by variously combining and securitizing already issued debt, adding another layer of indebtedness, which makes possible significant credit expansion in the financial markets. Overspeculation, particularly in collateralized debt obligations, is what led to the 2008 crash, and subsequent bailouts by the Fed were required to save both shadow banks and regular banks from the resulting credit crunch.[17]

***

The instability of modern bank money created by lending on a fractional reserve basis cannot be blamed on lending itself, which is an essential economic function. Credit and debt are not the problem. What compounds the burden of lending is not the repayment of principal; it is rather the additional payment of interest over principal, where fairness and justice come into question. What is a just rate of interest? Once upon a time, the debt burdens imposed by banks and lenders were called usury, and severely condemned; usury is still outlawed in many Muslim countries under Sharia law. Since the creation of money involves little or no labor or materials and only minimal infrastructure, and since the cost of labor and materials sets the economic value for goods and services, the money of account which bankers create 'out of nothing' appears in itself to have little if any intrinsic or commodity value; its only value comes from the collateral to which it is tied. Unlike, say, gold or silver coins, loans can be issued at little or no cost. Since its invention by the goldsmiths in London in the seventeenth century, modern bankers' credit-debt money lent on a fractional reserve basis has almost entirely displaced traditional commodity money—the coins of the sovereign. Traditional sovereigns—including monarchs, republics, and municipal corporations, evolving into nation states—since the eighteenth century found themselves facing an independent financial elite wielding unprecedented economic power based on the creation of debt-money by bank lending. This new financial power gradually came to rival if not dominate the state itself.

Monetary sovereignty, first stolen from the sovereign by private bankers in Britain in the eighteenth century, was stolen as well from the new republican governments, which replaced monarchies in the wake of the American and French Revolutions, and after World War I. This occurred partly because the monetary power of the old sovereigns was already limited. It extended only to standardizing by coinage one or another already preexisting commodity (usually gold, silver, or copper) as legal tender acceptable in taxes. To this end, coins of the realm were minted with the imprimatur of the sovereign and the value they represented was stamped upon them. This eliminated the awkward process of sifting and weighing raw and often impure metals in order to complete transactions and settle accounts, making coins enormously convenient.

But even this coinage by sovereigns was not yet the creation of money; it represented instead the rationalization of preexisting money into a standardized and more reliable form. Sovereigns did not create gold; they only repackaged it. Money can be defined as the most convenient medium of exchange which is accepted in final payment, and that, until recent times, has usually been found in some commodity form, that is, cash. All the traditional state could do in such circumstances was to privilege and streamline some already existing medium of exchange for final payment, some kind of cash, which over time sorted out to be mostly gold or silver. That was the limit of its power. It was the goldsmiths of the seventeenth century, as we shall see in the next chapter, who invented a way to actually create money 'out of thin air,' as the cliche goes, by fractional reserve banking. If authority over money is to be fully restored to the sovereign today, the sovereign will have to claim this new power as well to actually create money, in addition to the old power to merely shape and regulate and manage it. The question, as we shall see, is how that is to be done.

It is noteworthy that there are no significant material and labor costs for the creation of money of account by bank lending. It takes place simply on the basis of an idea, an intentional agreement between creditor and borrower, subsequently objectified in a loan contract. Money is created for the borrower, but only under the obligation of future repayment to the lender, and with the backing of productive assets as collateral. The creation of the money itself, as we have seen, is only a bookkeeping entry in the borrower's record made by the bank, whether by the stroke of a pen or the click of a computer key. The newly created money magically appears in the deposit account of the borrower: creation *ex nihilo*.

Can anything justify the interest rates charged by the private banking monopoly for providing what ought to be a public service? The conventional answer today, as in medieval times, points to the risk which lenders run of default by borrowers as the justification for interest. There are, however, mitigating factors today which significantly reduce risk not available in earlier times. Medieval creditors, like modern creditors, would have had (or should have had) as backing for any loan adequate collateral put up by the borrower (property, equipment, buildings, livestock, crops, inventory, etc.). After all, they were lending out their own money, not creating it. But for medieval bankers, collateral wasn't enough. They had to face the uncertainties of medieval life, which far exceeded those of modern life. Actual money (gold and silver) was scarce. It was easy to steal and untraceable. Insurance was expensive and often unavailable. Exchanges at a distance were slow and insecure. Information was hard to come by or verify. Wars, famines, plagues, bandits, armies, pirates, and other disruptions were far more common as everyday threats than they have been in recent times. Most important, perhaps, state power itself was limited and fragmented, and legal recourse was often unavailable or unreliable. In their world, medieval bankers were mostly on their own, and they were putting their own money at risk, so they had little choice but to charge high interest rates.

Bankers today are no longer on their own, and more importantly, they are no longer putting their own money at risk. Unlike medieval bankers, they have fewer risks to run. They have access to insurance, mathematical algorithms, and information technologies far more accurate in identifying and minimizing risk than anything available to medieval lenders. They enjoy the stability of networks coordinated by central banks. They benefit not only from legal protections by strong, commercially oriented governments, and from stable legal systems, but also from loan guarantees, central banks, and other government resources which stand ready to bail them out. Perhaps most of all, they enjoy state-sanctioned monopoly power over the issuance of debt-money, backed by their holdings of government debt, which is in turn backed by the taxing power of the state. They do not need or have the money they lend; they create it in the process of lending it. Some of these protections are now being extended to shadow bankers as well. All of this would have been a dream for medieval bankers.

Banks (that is, their owner-investors) are the first beneficiaries of the money they create by lending, but anyone who can be a creditor, who has money to lend—derived, say, from an inheritance, or business profits, or gifts, or theft, or somehow otherwise obtained, or even if it is borrowed—also benefits. Creditors are able to invest their profits more accurately and productively thanks to the benchmarks set by current bank rates, which provide standards of expected (and predictable) returns. As a result of the bankers' monopoly power to set interest rates, and the dominance of large banks within that monopoly, including shadow banks, a relatively small number of creditors are able to profit under normal circumstances (with a steadily productive economy) with little risk from the debts they hold. They are able to routinely extract excess wealth from the mass of borrowers, who have nowhere else to go for the credit they need. Creditors are able to appropriate and reinvest for themselves the interest paid to them by borrowers, while borrowers must labor (produce) that much more to pay it all back. All of this happens every day as a matter of ordinary business practice; it is what keeps the economy going.

The difficulty with credit-debt money is not that money is directly created by debt. The difficulty is that the excess or usurious rates of interest bankers are able to charge for this debt. "What is wrong with the current system," writes monetary critic Ellen Brown, "is not that money is advanced as a credit against the borrower's promise to repay but that the interest on this advance accrues to private banks that gave up nothing of their own to earn it."[18] The obligation to repay the principal is not in dispute. What is in dispute is what valid costs, if any, the borrower may owe the creditor beyond the actual expenses of the transaction. What effort or labor, what reason, justifies such extra costs? Should money not be a public good, rather than a private monopoly?

Shouldn't public goods be shared at cost, and not for profit? Wouldn't a national public banking system serve the needs and purposes of modern money creation, without the onerous levy of interest transferring wealth from borrowers to creditors? Should not the proven power of fractional reserve lending to multiply credit be dedicated to public benefit rather than private profit? Should not genuine popular sovereignty seek justice, or the public good, in the distribution of wealth? Should not the people direct their representatives to ensure the just distribution to them of their own money, as a public good? Is money not a credit against any goods and services that are for sale? Is not the just distribution of money identical to the just distribution of credit? Is a credit not a debt? Don't the resources which money is spent to consume need to be replenished? Don't borrowers need to repay their debts? Isn't it social justice to labor to replace what you consume? Shouldn't credit granted be commensurate with the ability to replace what is consumed, or to repay? Classic nineteenth century American populists raised and pursued such questions more thoroughly, perhaps, than anyone else. The chapters which follow outline their struggle for monetary justice in the context of current monetary practices and alternatives.

NOTES

1. James Chen, "Basel Accords: Purpose, History, and Member Countries," *Investopedia* 27 (April 2022): https://www.investopedia.com/terms/b/basel_accord.asp.

2. See Richard Werner, "How do Banks Create Money and Why Can Other Firms Not Do the Same? An Explanation for the Coexistence of Lending and Deposit Taking," in the *International Review of Financial Analysis* 36 (December 2014): 71–77; see also, Michael McLeay, Amar Radia, and Ryland Thomas, "Money Creation in the Modern Economy," Bank of England, *Quarterly Bulletin*, Q1, 2014; see also, Josh Ryan-Collins, Tony Greenham, Richard Werner, and Andrew Jackson, *Where Does Money Come From: A Guide to the UK Monetary and Banking System* (London: New Economics Foundation, 2011).

3. Richard Werner, "A Lost Century of Economics: Three Theories of Banking and the Conclusive Evidence," *International Review of Financial Analysis* 46 (July 2016): 361–79 https://www.sciencedirect.com/science/article/pii/S1057521915001477.

4. Ibid.

5. Ibid.

6. Ibid.

7. Ibid.

8. The modern reserve requirements for banking are evident in this report: Jeb Hensarling and Michael Solon, "Regulators May Sink America's Banks: A Credit-Tightening Increase on Capital Standards Won't Help the American Economy," T*he Wall Street Journal*, June 22, 2023, https://www.wsj.com/articles/regulators-may-sink-americas-banks-credit-economy-federal-reserve-crisis-4ccf1dc?mod=opinion_lead_pos5.

9. Ibid.

10. Richard Werner, "Can Banks Individually Create Money Out of Nothing? The Theories and the Empirical Evidence," Elsevier: *International Review of Financial Analysis* 36 (December 2014): 1–19, https://www.sciencedirect.com/science/article/pii/S1057521914001070.

11. See Charles Goodhart, and Meinhard Jensen, "Currency School versus Banking School: An Ongoing Confrontation," *Economic Thought* 4, no. 2 (2015): 20–31, https://eprints.lse.ac.uk/64068/1/Currency%20School%20versus%20Banking%20School.pdf.

12. Joseph Huber, "Currency vs. Banking Teachings: A Frame of Reference of Lasting Relevance to Modern Money Systems," Sovereign Money: Website for Monetary Systems Analysis and Reform, https://sovereignmoney.site/1-currency-versus-banking-teachings.

13. Michael Kumhof and Jaromir Benes, "The Chicago Plan Revisited," International Monetary Fund: *IMF Working Papers*, Working Paper WP12/202, August

2012, https://www.imf.org/en/Publications/WP/Issues/2016/12/31/The-Chicago-Plan-Revisited-26178.

14. Charles Goodhart and Meinhard Jensen, "Currency School versus Banking School: An Ongoing Confrontation, *Economic Thought* 4, no. 2 (2015): 20–31), https://eprints.lse.ac.uk/64068/1/Currency%20School%20versus%20Banking%20School.pdf.

15. See Richard Teitelbaum, "Conspiracy Theorists Ask 'Who Owns the New York Fed?' Here's the Answer," *Institutional Investor* (February 24, 2020), https://www.institutionalinvestor.com/article/b1kh4p10qysrhv/Conspiracy-Theorists-Ask-Who-Owns-the-New-York-Fed-Here-s-the-Answer.

16. By this I mean that private bankers invented fractional reserve banking—the key mechanism of modern bank money—in the seventeenth century. See Adrian Kuzminski, *The Ecology of Money: Debt Growth and Sustainability* (Lanhan, Lexington Books, 2013), chapter 4, "The Financial Revolution."

17. See Zoltan Polzar et al., "Shadow Banking" (New York: Federal Reserve Bank of New York, Staff Report No. 458, revised, July 2012).

18. Ellen Hodgson Brown, *The Web of Debt: The Shocking Truth of Our Money System* (Baton Rouge, Third Millenium Press, 2007), 404.

Chapter 2

The Creation of Money

Capitalism, as understood in this work, is the production of goods and services under private ownership to sell at a profit in a public market based on supply and demand. Profit is the surplus of money earned in sales over money spent in production (e.g., costs of raw materials, labor, equipment, energy, etc.). Loss is the opposite, a deficit of money earned relative to money spent. Capitalism requires more or less free (non-monopolistic) markets insofar as accurate prices can be determined only through open exchanges among many buyers and many sellers. A functioning market requires a medium of exchange as well. It cannot function—it cannot be a market—without money.

Imagine a flea market or swap meet, with hundreds of vendors selling a wide variety of items, and hundreds of customers. Without a medium of exchange, or money of some kind, there would be no unit of pricing, no common measure of exchange value, no easy way to settle transactions. I might go to the flea market to find a shirt I need, but, absent money, I would have to bring some more or less equivalent item I was willing to part with—say a chicken—in hopes of exchanging a chicken for a shirt. Success would require, as economists like to say, an unlikely double-coincidence: finding both someone willing to exchange a shirt for a chicken and someone willing to exchange a chicken for a shirt.

Money changes all that. It mediates between sellers and buyers. Instead of having to find a double-coincidence to make an exchange at the flea market, money allows any buyer to make any exchange with any seller, and vice-versa. Money can be almost any physical object, as we have seen, as long as it is accepted as a token of value in current payment to close a transaction. It can have an intrinsic value, like gold or silver, or no intrinsic value at all, like paper bills or numbers on a computer screen. It can have the official sanction of the state, making it legal tender, like the shekels of Sumerian cities, the coins of Roman and Chinese emperors, medieval monarchs, Civil War greenbacks, and Federal Reserve Notes, among many others. Or it can have merely the customary sanction of community consensus behind it, like cattle, wampum, beaver pelts, cigarettes, pearls, or any number of other items which have been historically used as media of exchange in various communities without official state sanction.

Whether it has intrinsic value or not, and whether it has state sanction or not, money at its most basic, is any evident item, more or less unproblematic, which is widely accepted among a community of buyers and sellers to complete their transactions. Even a computer entry is not nothing—it has to be visible on a screen to the right people at the right time to be recognized and used. Money is any such token accepted by a seller from a buyer, usually because the seller expects to use it in turn, when he or she becomes a buyer, to exchange it for something he or she may need. Money, as a token, is a comparative or relative measure, set mainly by supply and demand, of products and services available in the marketplace. It is in effect a credit, or IOU, held by the bearer, immediately redeemable against whatever goods and services are for sale. As monetary theorist Frederick Soddy puts it, "[T]he monetary system of distributing wealth does so because of the power it confers upon individuals *not* to possess but to be *owed* wealth to which they are entitled. . . . Money is not wealth even to the individual, but the evidence that the owner of the money has *not* received the wealth to which he is entitled, and that he can demand it at his own convenience." The wealth which is owned to the bearers of money Soddy calls "virtual wealth."[1]

Money allows for a wide range of comparisons not otherwise possible between goods and services, out of which in any market emerges a price point for any item. This is its approximate exchange value, the current average of offers or bids for an item among many buyers and sellers in the market. Price discovery requires a more or less transparent market, one where buyers can freely enter and circulate, and bid against one another for how much to pay the sellers for their products. Exchange values fluctuate with the fluctuations of the market, but at any given moment a prevailing price for any specific item can usually be discovered or reasonably estimated. The more transparency exists, the narrower the range of the price point. In a barter economy, on the other hand, where no money exists, there is no mechanism by which to measure and compare items offered by sellers against bids made by buyers, and so no price point at all can emerge; as a result, there is nothing we can call a market.

Markets don't make possible the existence of money; money makes possible the existence of markets, and thereby a capitalistic economy. Market exchange lies at the heart of capitalism, and at the heart of market exchange lies money. Money is something an individual can own or possess. A market is distinguished from barter by its use of money to clear goods and services; barter has no mechanism to clear exchanges between buyers and sellers and constitutes no market. A market is a clearing house mediated by money.

Money is a token of an accepted or agreed-upon imagined value, which it symbolically represents. The buyer offers the token, and the seller accepts it, not for its intrinsic worth, but because both understand it symbolically as a representation of a claim which the seller can use in turn to buy goods and services at the market.

Market economies have been the rule in most of recorded human history, from the earliest ancient city states in Mesopotamia and the Near East, up until modern times. Over thousands of years, precious metals, if available, often evolved into the monies of choice in many places. The silver shekel (a weight, not a coin) was already the principal monetary unit in Sumerian city states. When money, beginning at least mythically with Croesus in the sixth century BCE, was coined by sovereigns and accepted for taxes, it enjoyed the imprimatur of the state; but at the same time coins circulated independently as commodities, often outside the sovereign realm which issued them. Their commodity price helped fix their value as coins. Commercial profits—taken at any point of exchange—were the main source of accumulated wealth, but the last word in the settlement of accounts, when insisted upon, traditionally remained metallic currencies, preeminently silver and gold.

The great drawback of gold and silver and other commodity monies suitable for exchange is that they first have to be discovered in nature, and then mined and refined and otherwise processed before they can conveniently be used. There is no reason to doubt that these monies grew out of long histories of trial and error. Commodity money is naturally found money, so to speak, and it is in relatively fixed supply at any given time. The result of this circumstance has been a chronic lack of money, which has constrained economic activity in most pre-industrial economies based on commodity monies. Most goods and services in traditional societies were produced and consumed locally, through local markets, and only supplemented (and not dominated by) longer distance trade. The predominantly rural pre-industrial economies functioned on a primitive renewable basis. Dependent on animal, wind, and water power, they could produce only limited amounts of energy. What concentrated accumulation did occur came mostly through arbitrage, whenever merchants were able to buy low and sell high, mostly in long distance trade.[2] Commodity monies and especially precious metals likely arose in this context.

Finance in an economy based on commodity money is a zero-sum game. A dollar lent out is a dollar subtracted from the assets of the lender. In this situation, one can only borrow from the present, and not from the future. One can only borrow from the stock of already existing accumulated money, if one can get access to it. It is credit which potentially transforms this situation. When fully developed in a banking system, credit (which is also debt) can turn zero-sum commodity money into the win-win money of account. Money of account is a representation of commodity money; it is a promise of commodity money, not commodity money itself, but insofar as it circulates as a means of payment alongside commodity money, it can significantly expand the money supply, the supply of what Soddy called outstanding claims against resources due to the bearer.

Borrowing from the future requires a new and different kind of money—money which can be created out of nothing; money which expands, and not only redistributes, the existing money supply. This is imagined real money which can be spent now and repaid later. But although commodity money and money of account recording debts, including interest, both appear in the earliest written historical records, from the second and third millennia BCE, found in ancient Sumerian cities,[3] they should not be confused with the later forms taken by both commodity monies and debt. The silver shekel was the unit of commodity money, mainly used in long distance trade by merchants in Sumerian cities, but until coinage was invented thousands of years later (traditionally attributed to Croesus, King of Lydia in the sixth century BCE), commodity monies, even precious metals, remained inconvenient, awkward, of uncertain quality, and risky to use. The lack of coinage, and the difficulties of measuring and assaying raw and uncertain quantities of silver or other commodities in final payment to close a transaction, indicates that commerce would have been a specialized business, with markets limited to relatively few items, compared to later periods. Merchants were few in number and focused on rare or luxurious items usually not locally available. There were surely markets, and temple and palace storehouses, but this was far from a more generalized, everyday consumer society with real money in most people's pockets and a wide variety of competing goods and services for sale.

Some authors, including David Graeber and Michael Hudson, have seen the essence of money as debt writ large in the Sumerian experience.[4] Graber writes that "our standard account of monetary history is precisely backwards. We did not begin with barter, discover money, and then eventually develop credit systems. It happened precisely the other way around. What we now call virtual money came first. Coins came much later, and their use spread only unevenly, never completely replacing credit systems. Barter, in turn, appears to be largely a kind of accidental byproduct of the use of coinage or paper money."[5] Hudson emphasizes not only the importance of debt in the origin of money in the ancient Near East, but the redeeming feature of its practice—codified in Sumerian and later Babylonian and in Talmudic law—of periodic cancellation of debts, or debt jubilees. He writes, "By limiting the consequences of unpaid rural debts to only temporary duration, Mesopotamia's restoration of economic order avoided the problem that developed in classical antiquity, when debt became a wedge pushing economies further and further out of balance. Looking over the broad sweep of history, debt strains have never been dealt with in so comprehensive a way as in Mesopotamia at the very onset of the debt dynamic."[6]

It might be doubted whether a cancellation of debts in an economy where interest on debt denominated in grain was set at 33.3%, and interest on debt denominated in silver at 20%,[7] was other than an act of desperation, which might, at the succession of a new king, take the form of a prudent need to establish some good will. Interest rates were punishing and debt slavery was common, and debts were only canceled for farmers who borrowed grain from temples or palaces, and not for those who owed silver to merchants for commodities, perhaps because farmers were also needed as soldiers to defend their cities. The creditor–debtor relationship for most people in ancient Mesopotamia did not involve the kind of bank-money that was only created much later by modern fractional reserve lending. Mesopotamian debt appears to have been traditional or simple debt, lent on a 100% deposit basis. Grain was stored in temple or palace granaries from the previous harvest, it appears, and its advance to tide over farmers was made on condition of its full replacement, plus interest, by the farmers after the next harvest. The etymology of the word 'interest' in Sumerian and other ancient languages (like Greek) comes from the natural increase of fertile plants and animals, such as the calf which might be expected of a cow. There is no reason to think that the clay tablets, which registered debts on account were themselves ever used as money, as well as the grain or silver they represented. There is no evidence that clay tablets were ever issued on other than a one-to-one basis to the commodity money they represented.

Although commodity money and debt appeared in the Near East by the end of the third millennium BCE, their latent possibilities took a long time to develop. Sumerian city states, and subsequent Near Eastern kingdoms and empires, largely failed to break through deep class divisions between priests, rulers, and merchants, on the one hand, and farmers and peasants on the other. The latter group were the debtors, the former the creditors. Centralized state credit perpetuated a pattern of dependency with little or no opportunity for debtors to break out of the cycle. Control of the granaries or other storage facilities gave priests and monarchs, with the assistance of merchants, a choke hold over farmers. Farmers' security depended on receiving, as needed, grain from last year's surplus before this year's crops could be harvested. This meant that agriculture and the economy it supported had to operate on a wholesale basis. Producers would request grain from, or bring grain to, the temple, depending on their circumstances, where the price was most likely set. Instead of a free and open market, with many farmers or producers negotiating with many buyers or consumers, and a price set by supply and demand, the temple and palace storage complexes which controlled keeping accounts appear to have set monopoly prices and terms of exchange by imposing high interest rates (33.3% on grain) they demanded for their own purposes. Here we see perhaps an early prototype of state capitalism.

The next monetary revolution came much later, with the invention of coinage of precious metals in the sixth century BCE in what is now Anatolia, which was then the borderland between Near Eastern and Greek cultures. Coins appeared at about the same time in northern India and China. The invention of coins destroyed the monetary monopoly hitherto held by temple-palace complexes typical of Near Eastern empires. Under the centralized temple-palace storage system, we may presume accounts were held at the temple, where debtors (probably illiterate) were informed of their options. Money was issued as debt, measured in grain, and similarly collected in return, with interest. Coins, however, once invented, were a different matter. There is some evidence that coins were first struck by popular leaders (usurping kings, rebels, or tyrants) in competition with traditional elites.[8] Coins (whether gold, silver, copper, even iron, or some other metal) had the advantage of dispensing with the laborious evaluation and processing (separating, refining, weighing) of varied, disorganized, and unpredictable collections of precious bulk metals, or bullion, previously required to complete payment of transactions. Coins are specie, or standardized metallic tokens, usually minted with the stamp of the sovereign, along with a mark of their comparative value.

The invention of coinage radically democratized money. It made possible for the first time what might be called decentralized retail commercial activity, as opposed to the centralized wholesale distribution of goods and services characteristic of earlier New Eastern states, whether practiced by temples and palaces or by low-distance merchants. The lack of coinage ensured that transactions had to go through state institutions or specialized merchants. They alone were in a position to determine the agreed upon amount of bulk metals needed to complete transactions. But since the value of minted coins was self-evident by their weight and stamp, the middleman between buyer and seller was eliminated.

The invention of coinage was the revolutionary herald of a new commercial age. In Athens particularly, but in other Greeks cities as well, more grain was imported than locally grown. This was possible because the rich Laurian silver mines of the Athenians allowed them to pay for grain and other imports. The mines were developed by private entrepreneurs who purchased leases from the state for extracting and smelting the silver. The minting of silver coins, introduced by the tyrant Peisistratus, created a generalized cash economy. Debts and other obligations could be paid in cash, that is, coin. The payment of citizens by the state for public services (serving on juries, in assemblies, and other government bodies) further distributed the new money. Instead of the central state accounting of the Sumerians and Babylonians, with money apparently under total elite control of priests and kings, anyone in Athens and other Greek cities could do their own accounting by managing their own coins. They could spend, borrow, lend, and invest as they saw fit. To guarantee the safekeeping of money, to concentrate larger sums, and to facilitate lending, simple banking, unknown in Mesopotamia, was invented. Bankers took in deposits and made loans on their own, or in conjunction with their depositors. The new coined money for the first time circulated freely and directly among individuals, without passing through central state control, making possible countless independent economic exchanges. Money had become democratized.[9]

The Roman world vastly expanded this monetized commercial economy, extending it well into three continents. In contrast to the state bureaucracies of the ancient Near East, the Romans, like the Greeks, developed an economy of private enterprise. The wealth of elite Roman families, the patrician class, was rooted in vast property holdings accumulated through centuries of imperial conquest. Although prohibited by law from engaging in business activity, their ability to lend money (to invest) made them the major source of capital. The second class of Roman society, the knights, the equivalent of the productive middle class, were open to business enterprises, as were other free Romans as well. The Roman administration, like the Athenian, preferred not to develop commercial state enterprises, if it could avoid it, but chose instead to contract them out to individuals. Business enterprises were organized as publican societies, or quasi-corporations—organizations based on limited liability for their shareholders. Financial historian William Goetzmann quotes Polybius's observation that "virtually every citizen in Rome participated in the business of government contracts, implying that membership in publican societies was widespread. . . . Corporate-like institutions owned collectively among hundreds or perhaps thousands of investors offered a novel form of business venture; one in which investors were not directly involved in the activities of the company but instead were passive recipients of profits according to their ownership shares."[10]

After the Second Punic war, the silver and gold mines of Iberia, hitherto the province of Carthage, passed to the Romans. Coins minted from Iberian silver and gold paid Roman soldiers and spread through the economy, replicating, on a larger scale, the advantage in coinage already exhibited by the ancient Athenians. On this steady cash basis, the publican societies and banks and a mature superstructure of lending and borrowing was developed. Goetzmann sums it up as follows:

> The most remarkable thing about finance in the ancient world is that basically all of the financial tools were developed by early societies of the Near East and the eastern Mediterranean before the current era: financial contracts, mortgages,

> equity and debt instruments, commercial courts, merchant law, private corporations, banks, and banking systems. Even more sophisticated conceptual tools emerged, such as financial planning, models of economic growth, the mathematics of compound interest, and empirical records to memorialize and analyze price trends through history.[11]

There is one fundamental financial tool Goetzmann leaves out, and it is arguably the distinguishing factor between ancient and modern commercial societies: the literal creation of money out of nothing through fractional reserve banking. As far as scholars seem able to determine, the ancient economies of the West functioned on a cash basis, that is, on the basis of coined money, or specie.[12] Money lent out was coin, even when debts and other transactions were represented in bookkeeping entries in place of actual transfers of coins. The bookkeeping entries stood in a direct one-to-one relationship to the coins they represented. The disruptive idea that the same coins might be lent simultaneously to more than one individual—the basis, as we shall see, of modern fractional reserve banking—seems to have been inconceivable in ancient, medieval, or even early modern times. As long as the accounting of real money, or coin, remained on a 100% basis, the money in circulation—silver, gold, copper, and so forth—was a natural substance which had to be found, or discovered, in nature, hence the importance of the Laurion and Iberian and other mines. The growth of the economy depended directly on the natural availability of such metals—a fact made evident again when the discovery of gold and silver resources in America in the sixteenth century helped fuel an economic boom in Europe.

The idea that money could actually be created was an invention not of ancient but of modern private bankers, which in large part explains why it's still under their control. Traditional commodity money, it should be emphasized, was never created; it was discovered and refined. It may not have grown on trees, but we might say it grew in the earth, like gold or silver, in the water like beaver pelts, or even in the sea, like cowrie shells or pearls. Its supply could be increased only by the discovery of new sources, and much early modern exploration by the European powers, from Columbus on, was famously motivated by the search for gold and silver. Since the time of Croesus, monarchs, city states, republics, and other sovereign powers had been minting precious metal coins, or specie, primarily out of gold and silver, which they spent on armies, navies, bureaucracies, palaces, harbors, roads, estates, and other works, and which they took back in payment of taxes, guaranteeing a demand for their money.

The king may put his image and stamp on the coins produced in his mint, and take them back in taxes, but he is not creating a new currency, only standardizing the form of an existing commodity (say, gold or silver) already widely if informally used in final payments. The principal benefit of such a currency does not necessarily go to the king or queen, but to whoever controls the production, exchange, storage, and distribution of gold. Historically in early modern Europe this turned out to be the early bankers, the Fuggers, Medicis, Bardis, and others. The kings were chronically in debt to the bankers, and frequently defaulted. They were unable to control their own currencies.

To maintain the commodity money system, premodern states were forced to accumulate and recycle whatever precious metals they could find. Since states didn't know how to create rather than discover commodity money, they had to earn it, find it, or even steal it. Commodity money was highly variable. It could be scarce, and credit correspondingly hard to come by, or relatively abundant, allowing easier credit. Ancient and medieval bankers dealt either in precious metals, or in limited paper notes or certificates (like bills of exchange) which directly and uniquely represented the metals in question. Any particular note was fixed as representing one particular amount of precious metal. Gold and silver (and copper, bronze, etc.) had evolved early on to absorb a diverse field of local commodities previously used as means of exchange (salt, cattle, grain, jewelry, and later tally sticks, wampum, beaver pelts, etc.). Over time, and in most places, precious metals when available tended to become the basic forms of commodity money, absorbing the functions of their less convenient predecessors, but their accumulation always remained dependent upon natural and unpredictable conditions, and varied markedly from place to place.

Abundance and scarcity of money each had its consequences. The relative abundance of commodity money allowed that it could be borrowed at reasonable rates, while its relative scarcity drove up rates, which were widely resented and condemned as usurious.[13] Many borrowers, even in good times, often fell into debt bondage, having to surrender property or labor to their creditors, an important reason economic growth remained stagnant, or barely perceptible, over long historical periods. Debtor rebellions decrying usury were a feature of the more developed economies found in ancient and early modern eras. Early modern creditors, such as Renaissance bankers, were, like most ancient lenders, mainly private individuals who pushed back against the charge of usury. Increased commerce and larger wars, Renaissance bankers argued, demanded increased credit. Without some kind of compensation for putting their assets at greater risk by lending them out, and lacking any kind of government backing, they not unreasonably demanded some kind of reliable consideration—for which, they argued, the most convenient mechanism was to charge whatever interest borrowers were willing to pay.

If interest rates are conceded any legitimacy, and not wholly rejected as usurious, the question becomes what is and what is not a usurious rate of interest. Extreme critics had denounced any interest at all as usurious, but moderates agonized over whether any interest might be justified, and how much. As long as no satisfactory answer to this question was offered, it was gradually realized that any rate of interest might just as well be justified as rejected. Its critics failed to outlaw usury because they could not define it, except to identify usury with interest, a position too extreme to be tenable. In the end, to get the credit they desired, what most Western countries once regarded as usurious practices came to be accepted as natural and normal and were finally legitimized in law. Today they are business as usual.

***

The insight that money could be created rather than discovered came rather late in the game. To whom the credit should go may be disputed, and a step-by-step account of how it happened is yet to be written and remains beyond the scope of this work, but a plausible case can be made that the London goldsmiths of the mid-seventeenth century, whether or not they first invented money creation, were the ones who put the idea into circulation, at least in London circles, and laid the precedents which were later followed. They found that the gold entrusted to their safekeeping was but infrequently reclaimed by depositors, and rarely, if ever, all at once; they also found that the certificates or promissory notes they exchanged in return for the gold deposited in their vaults were themselves circulating among third parties, in place of the actual gold they represented, as a currency used to settle commercial transactions. They were a way to bypass commodity money without abandoning it. These certificates appeared to be (and were accepted as) equivalent to the gold they represented because they promised boldly that they could be redeemed at any time by the bearer for the equivalent amount of real gold in the goldsmith's vault.

Because paper certificates, or notes, were superior to actual gold in important ways—given their convenience as lightweight, easily stored, and readily transferred units of exchange—they came to be overwhelmingly preferred in place of gold itself for most financial transactions, including final settlements. Earlier promissory notes, such as merchants' bills of exchange, were encumbered by personal endorsements, fixed for specific sums, and good only over limited periods of time. The goldsmiths' notes, by contrast, were entirely anonymous (payment was simply due to the bearer), had convenient uniform denominations, had no expiration date, and therefore were widely accepted in final payment, ending a transaction—the ultimate mark of money—in place of 'real' money: gold or silver. They triumphed because their liquidity, efficiency, and convenience was vastly superior to that of the physical gold they nonetheless continued to represent.

While depositors could not redeem more than a fraction of their certificates at once, the likelihood of them having to do so at any given time remained very low. This curious state of affairs enabled the expansion of the meaning of money from being a commodity, which had to be laboriously discovered, extracted, and processed before it could be used as final payment, to an obligation—an interpersonal act of the imagination made manifest in a token of the commodity itself—a piece of paper or note with negligible, if any, commodity value at all. Gradually, but steadily, the arduous effort of finding, mining, shipping, and minting limited quantities of gold or silver into coins was relieved by the ease of simply printing and signing paper certificates representing gold, produced on the spot at nominal expense, in quantities limited only by the demand for credit.

The public's preference for gold certificates over actual gold in transactions also meant that borrowers were happy to accept gold certificates in place of actual gold for the loans they sought from the goldsmiths. This allowed the goldsmiths to issue many more gold certificates as loans to borrowers than the amount of gold they actually held in reserve to back up these new certificates. As long as most holders of gold certificates (whether original depositors of gold or new borrowers) did not demand real gold in return for cashing in their certificates, the effective amount of money in circulation remained much higher than it otherwise would have been. This was the essence of the modern financial revolution.

Before bankers invented how to create money, rather than just lend out money they already had, how much could be lent was closely limited by the amount of coin in circulation. Traditional promissory notes, having little or no exchange value in themselves, tended not to circulate but to be held until redeemed in specie. Since no new commodity money was being reliably created, or only slowly and laboriously at best with the occasional discovery of new mines, the usurious rates which were attached to loans based on commodity monies meant that at any point more money was owned than could be repaid, making loans a risky and frowned upon business. Before the London goldsmiths of the seventeenth century, money could be lent out *only once at a time*. The goldsmiths learned how to create money by finding a way to *relend the same money to many people at the same time, over and over again*, creating a one-to-many correlation between lenders and borrowers, and gold and its certificates.

This vastly expanded both the money supply and the profits to be gained from interest. As long as borrowers were confident of productively investing their money, they were happy to take on more debt. It turned out that the appetite for debt in the wake of the financial and industrial revolutions far exceeded everyone's wildest estimates. Vast quantities of new debt allowed for unprecedented investment in productive enterprises which unleashed nothing less, I have argued elsewhere, than the industrial revolution itself.[14] Creditors continued to exploit debtors, but as long as the economy continued to grow fast enough to increase the returns to both debtors and creditors, everyone benefited. Creditors got much richer, of course, but debtors made real gains as well.

While credit was already well developed in ancient times and survived the collapse of the complex commercial economy of the Romans, even at its best it remained directly tethered to its cash basis. Prior to the invention of fractional reserve banking, credit could not increase but only temporally redistribute the money supply. Current savings were freed up to be lent and spent in the present in return for a promise by the borrower to replenish the creditor's savings in the future. Interest payments would appear to increase the cash supply, but their role as a hedge against the risk of default would seem to have minimized any such gains. The real increase in money supply in premodern financial systems, even with considerable credit, depended mainly on new discoveries of precious metals, the only practical source of real money, or cash.

The new credit paper money created by the goldsmiths upset the direct, one-to-one relationship in which the old commodity money stood in relation to the loans in which it was denominated. The old one-to-one relationship between coins and notes, taken for granted by promissory notes and bills of exchange, was replaced by a one-to-many relationship between coins and the notes invented by the goldsmiths. Previously, the intrinsic market value of gold (and silver and other metals) had ensured a direct and relatively stable relationship between coins and the products and services they could purchase. Both the amount of gold available and the amount of goods and services produced changed but slowly over time. By contrast, the easy issuance of multiple gold certificates with claims to the same gold—the goldsmiths' ingenious way of making one equal many—destabilized and disrupted the traditional direct relationship between money and what it could buy. Money in its new post-commodity form became a variable—an algebraic rather than arithmetical value—fluctuating with the ebbs and flows of borrowing and repayment.

The pretense which made the goldsmiths' audacious and ingenious fiction of multiple-single ownership plausible was the immediate redemption promised to any holder of a gold certificate of the actual physical gold specified on the face of the certificate. The odds of the gold being in the vault were not foolproof, it was perhaps understood, but they were very high, high enough, in fact, to dramatically minimize the risk of a bank run, which is all that mattered to most depositors. It was necessary in order for the fiction to work to believe (to accept or presume) the contradictory idea that multi-ownership was really single ownership for all practical purposes. The limitations and scarcity of real gold were overcome *in the imagination* by the calculation that the much more convenient paper certificates guaranteeing access to gold were 'as good as gold.' The certificates, the notes of the goldsmiths, insofar as they were promises for immediate commodity money on demand, turned out to be virtually if not really equivalent to actual money. They were good enough to be accepted and exchanged in place of the actual gold they represented. As long as people believed in the validity of the gold certificates, there was little need to test the faith.

The goldsmiths invented a machine for money creation, commonly called fractional reserve banking. It was conceived, in its original version, on the model of a single institution or bank, and only became systematic in recent times with the rise of banking networks, central banks, insurance, and government bailouts. The breakthrough was the recognition that loans did not need 100% reserves on the part of the lender, but only a much smaller percentage. The percentage of reserves to deposits has varied historically considerably, but holding 10% in reserves is often used as a generous rule of thumb, though reserve deposits were often even lower.[15] Goldsmiths and early bankers realized they could come to an agreement with their borrowers in which both parties presumed that a gold certificate or bank note represented an exclusive and direct claim to some actual amount of gold, when in fact it was not an exclusive and direct claim at all, but merely one of many potentially competing claims issued by the goldsmiths for exactly the same gold. Nevertheless, the contradictory fiction of *multiple single owners* was embraced as if it were a fact, as an article of faith. Borrowers and creditors alike were happy to accept the fiction insofar as both stood to benefit in the short run. After all, the risk of a run on any goldsmith's bank looked remote by comparison. Normally, 99% percent of the time, let us say, the certificates were redeemable without any difficulty, as depositors could see for themselves; only 1% of the time or less, it seemed, might something like a bank run be even imaginable. Mostly bank runs happened to other people in other times and other places, as one might easily believe. The prospect of a bank run became a speculative and remote risk, like being struck by lightning.

The invention of the fiction of money creation—a simple intentional human act—made the goldsmiths the first true bankers. Lending and borrowing, it turns out, do not in themselves exhaust the possibilities of banking. Medieval and renaissance bankers were constantly lending and borrowing, but they did not create money; like everyone else, they could only lend out what they already had or could reasonably be expected to provide. The goldsmiths by contrast were the first real money creators, and therefore the first modern bankers. Their working prototype of money creation through lending was the model perfected by the Bank of England (1694), and it has since spread around the world. Today, fractional reserve banking, as we saw in the last chapter, has evolved beyond keeping some gold coins in the vault to cover withdrawals. The equity or capital assets of the bank today, along with those of the banking system as a whole, form a much broader range and more flexible pool of reserves underwriting a bank's solvency, but the principle is the same.

When early bankers—the goldsmiths and their successors—realized that they could create money, they found they could dwarf the more limited commodity money of the king or sovereign. This private money creation at the expense of the sovereign allowed bankers (and creditors in general) to accrue enormous wealth and power by charging interest on what became a much-expanded number of loans. This credit money in due course became the virtual currency of the nation. In the modern age, even though republics based on popular sovereignty have mostly replaced sovereign monarchs, modern states have largely failed to recover the monopoly over money earlier sovereigns enjoyed. That monopoly has remained in the hands of the bankers. As a result, private interests have continued to own and profit from what was once the interest of the realm as a whole.

In brief, commodity money (preeminently gold and silver) is not created, we have maintained; rather it is discovered in nature to be a useful medium of exchange, and eventually refined and structured into its most convenient form, namely, coins or specie. Receipts, promissory notes, bills of exchange, loan contracts, and other representations or certificates of commodity money were traditionally presumed to stand in a direct relationship to the money they represented, so that a one dollar note, say, stood for one dollar of specie. The post-goldsmith bankers, as we have seen, upset this equation. They put commodity money largely out of circulation by persuading borrowers to accept the far more convenient anonymous certificates representing gold in place of the gold itself. Paper money replaced hard money for most purposes. It turned out that the ultimate limit on anonymous certificates or notes was not the gold that bankers held in their vaults but the number of viable borrowers among the public seeking credit. This turned out to be a large group whose demands for credit vastly expanded the earlier money supply. The new credit-debt money was denominated in the currency of the realm. It consisted mainly of paper money at first, mainly bank notes, and more recently money on account simply added to borrowers' deposits listed on their bank's legers, and transferred via checks rather than bank notes, supplemented by coins as cash as needed. The bankers' coup was complete.

Today precious metals have largely been relegated to the sidelines.[16] They play no significant role (except as small change) in monetary operations, though a vocal minority of gold bugs (inspired by the Austrian school) continue to call for a restoration of the gold standard. The one-time certificates of the goldsmiths have evolved into everyday currency, replacing precious metals (specie) in that role. Cash today in America and large parts of the world is the physical United States dollar, comprised of the paper bills known as the Federal Reserve notes. Dollars can be redeemed only in other dollars, never in gold or silver or anything else. In bank runs today depositors are seeking to convert money of account into what is now the medium of last resort for final payments—physical Federal Reserve notes which, like coins, can be grasped in the hand and retained under personal control, with no need of further redemption. One thinks of suitcases full of 'benjamins,' or $100 Federal Reserve notes, as used for many direct payments, sometimes of large amounts, particularly with organized crime, corrupt officials, terrorist or paramilitary groups, and others operating outside the banking system.

Fractional reserve banking, at its simplest, requires only that the lending bankers keep in reserve an amount of whatever constitutes the current form of commodity money, or cash, to cover withdrawals. Today the reserves are built into the banking system as a whole, as we've seen, with government backing. Lending is not a steady business, but one which waxes and wanes in light of economic prospects. The boom-and-bust cycle is necessarily built into the modern, money-creating finance system. Premodern, non-fractional lending could result in crises as well. There were financial panics in ancient Rome. But modern fracking reserve banking has greatly exaggerated this dynamic. The productivity which the loans demand from the economy in order to be repaid comes somewhat irregularly and unpredictably, not smoothly. Discoveries, innovations, disruptions, natural disasters, and other surprises may upset the best of plans, leading to defaults on loans and liquidations. That is part of normal economic life. What makes the process of booms and busts much more dramatic and disturbing, however, is the combination of modern fractional reserve banking with the usurious rates charged by the private banking monopoly.

***

It cannot be overstated that, from the late seventeenth century on, a new kind of created money became dominant in the West. This modern credit-debt money, or bank money, was a peculiar human invention, not an accident of nature. The older commodity monies which preceded it functioned as first order natural money. The invention of second-order, credit-debt human money evolved out of modifications to bills of exchange and other receipts or proxies for commodity monies. Over time they were refined into denominated, anonymous, freely circulating tickets, or paper bills, or notes. The financial revolution presaged by the goldsmiths was brought to a climax with the Bank of England. The goldsmiths had created a new mechanism which made possible a financial system of second-order credit-debt money in place of first-order commodity money. They did not invent credit, which has a long history, but they found a way, as we have seen, through fractional reserve banking, to multiply the credit they could extend far beyond the one-to-one correlation to cash, or hard money, which had hitherto constrained the amount of credit available at any one time. They succeeded in turning credit into money. Debt, previously a secondary contractual arrangement between individuals involving money, ended up functioning as money itself, and largely displaced its older commodity forms.

The goldsmiths had the idea of credit as money, but they did not turn it into a full-fledged monetary system. They operated as independent agents, and their notes had no legal or institutional endorsement. The first real credit-money system was established and eventually institutionalized only when the private investors who funded the Bank of England won a legal monopoly over the creation of the new money (credit money through fractional reserve lending) for the public, in return for assuming the national debt of the state. This monetary revolution made modern economic and financial practices possible. It allowed people, for the first time in human history, not only to use natural substances as money but to create money 'out of nothing.' With credit and money expansion no longer dependent on discoveries of gold and silver, it became possible to vastly increase the scope of lending, and to invest in and thereby dramatically increase current production on a scale hitherto impossible. It not only enabled the industrial revolution and modern (as opposed to feudal) society, but it also accelerated the unjustified transfer of wealth from debtors to creditors through usurious interest rates which applied to the new credit or bank money as much as they had applied to the old commodity money. It was a paradigm shift.

The Bank of England was established in 1694 by a consortium of private creditors under an act of Parliament. The new King of England, William III, was in dire need of funds to pursue war against Louis XIV in defense of his native Holland. In a deal between a group of private creditors and the British government, the new Bank would lend William £1.2 million put up by the creditors for his war at the rate of 8% plus expenses. "In return for lending at this low rate," as financial historian Christopher Hollis succinctly puts it, "the Bank received a number of privileges of which the most important was that it had the right to issue notes up to the extent of its loan to the Government 'under their common seal' on the security of the government. That is to say, it had the right to issue a £1 note; the holder of that note had the right to demand that the Bank give him cash for his note, but, if he made that demand, the Bank had the right to demand that the Government raise that £1 by taxation and repay £1 worth of debt to the Bank so that the Bank might repay its £1 to the note-holder."[17]

In this way, monopoly powers were given by an act of parliament to private investors to control the creation of money as credit, backed by the government's power of taxation. It allowed them to impose their own private tax on lending, now vastly expanded by fractional reserve banking, in the form of usurious interest rates. The Bank in this way gained control over the issuance of a novel and more powerful British currency. The Bank's influence in Parliament, as Hollis goes on to point out, was crucial. It was able to block any vote instructing the Government to fund William's war, thus forcing the monarch to borrow from the Bank. This dependency soon became permanent, and the Bank quickly went on to issue notes far in excess of the initial limitation of 1.2 million pounds, solidifying its power over money creation in England.

Alexander Hamilton later called this the 'English system,' and as a money creation mechanism it was unprecedented in world history. Even the bank of Amsterdam, which pioneered many modern banking techniques, operated on a full reserve, not a fractional reserve, basis. In Hamilton's words, "The Bank of England unites public authority and faith with private credit; and hence we see what a vast fabric of paper credit is raised on a visionary basis. Had it not been for this, England would never have found sufficient funds to carry on her wars; but with the help of this she has done, and is doing wonders."[18] The 'visionary basis' here is fractional reserve banking. Hamilton's aim was to establish a version of this system, with built-in lending at interest, in the United States. For the first time ever, in England, the taxing power of the state was used as a reserve fund backing a national debt held by private investors for their personal profit. This set the pattern for modern private banking. Seventeenth-century goldsmiths had discovered that they could lend out their notes in excess of their personal gold reserves. Now, with British pounds backed by a national debt, the banks, like the goldsmiths before them, were able to confidently lend out far more money than they had on deposit. They had gained an official legitimacy the goldsmiths could only have dreamt of. The result was an enormous expansion of private credit. This new and reliable credit was central to the British victories over the French in the wars of the eighteenth century, as Hamilton noted, leading to the rise of the British colonial empire, and the funding of what turned out to be the industrial revolution.

This British financial revolution may be the most underappreciated event in modern history. The unprecedented economic productivity it unleashed has transformed the planet. Along the way, long-standing objections to interest rates as usury were overridden. Interest was defended by bankers as the price of risk, and its fluctuating rate, they claimed, was naturally set according to the shifting needs of creditors and the varying demands of debtors. What could be fairer, they asked? They invoked Jeremy Bentham, whose pivotal essay "Defense of Usury"[19] argued that interest rates were legitimate and ought to be settled by a free market of supply and demand. Far from operating in a free market, however, the private banking system—then as now effectively a cartel run by the largest banks—exercises monopoly control over money creation and the interest rate. Banks are officially chartered institutions given the sole right to offer deposits, to invent money by making loans, to provide necessary accounting services, and to set interest rates on their loans, all for a profit. A bank operating under fractional reserve procedures brings money into existence every time it makes a loan, and the notes it issues are legal tender. Because it holds a monopoly over the money system, it can charge a monopoly priced interest rate for its product.

The rate of interest governs how the surplus of future production made possible by a loan is to be divided between creditors and debtors, with the former, in the wake of the financial revolution, in a stronger position to demand a larger share, as determined by the rate of interest they placed on their loans. The higher the rate of interest, the greater the portion of productive surplus which debtors must share with creditors; the lower the rate, the greater the portion which the debtors can keep for themselves. The ability of the banking monopoly to charge usurious rates on money it loans has ensured a massive, ongoing transfer of wealth from debtors to creditors. But why should a debtor be made liable to share a portion of the fruits of his or her labor beyond what is necessary to repay the principal—the amount actually borrowed—plus any natural or operational fees? If the money created by lending can be understood as an indispensable social utility, as properly a public function, it ought to be made available to the public at cost. But this did not happen.

The financial revolution in England instead kept the new power of money creation in the private hands where it had originated. The unearned benefits from that new credit money went into the hands of a small private financial elite of bank investors, who accumulated vast wealth and power from their monopoly over the money power, now legally sanctioned, leaving much of the population indebted and financially insecure, and more or less defrauded of the benefits of their borrowing. The debt-money of the bankers did an end run around the commodity monies previously issued by the sovereign. The human face of the sovereign (king, queen, or president) might still appear on coins and bills, but the ability of private bankers to multiply the credit of the sovereign to their exclusive benefit was firmly institutionalized, and increasingly taken for granted. The private tax of usurious interest rates imposed by bankers on money they learned to create in return for the availability of credit today was built into the very fabric of society, where it remains to this day.

Without credit no complex economy can function. Even in a simple local economy, with many uncomplicated direct exchanges, the merchant will often need to advance credit to the mechanic or the farmer on the basis of the latter's promise to produce the goods or harvest the crops in order to sell them on the market to repay the merchant's loan. Without having reliable credit available, productivity would regress to pre-industrial levels, and perhaps even to pre-commercial or subsistence levels. In the new system of credit-based bank money, old loans are continually being paid off as new ones are being taken out. Premodern commercial economies lacked such an institutionalized credit system. Each new venture normally had to find financing from scratch. Premodern banking remained limited to personal accumulations of commodity money. The modern economy by contrast can rely on sources of credit provided by modern banking, which allow it to carry a perpetual debt burden, as it must in order to function. Any debt, however, given the burden of usurious interest rates can become onerous, and polarize debtors and creditors. When credit became money in the wake of the financial revolution, the burden of interest which had always accompanied credit was only magnified.

***

What is the measure of the burden of usurious debt? The father of populist monetary theory, Edward Kellogg, was among the first to systematically question the private bankers' monopoly over debt money—the modern legacy of 'the English system' and the financial revolution it represented. In his posthumously published 1861 work, *A New Monetary System*, he writes, "The law of interest, or percentage on money, as much governs the rent or use of all property, and consequently the reward of labor, as the law of gravitation governs the descent of water. If the interest on money be too high, a few owners of capital will inevitably accumulate the wealth of products of the many."[20] How much can they accumulate? What is the measure of that accumulation? How can we calculate the burden? Here is Kellogg's answer: "Money loaned on interest or invested in property, is doubled in a certain length of time, determined by the rate of interest. When this rate is too high, it requires the principal to be doubled in so short a time, that the borrower is compelled to give all his surplus products as interest or rent; whereas, justice requires that he should pay only a moderate percentage for the use of capital, and himself retain the chief surplus of his labor."[21]

The following table illustrates the doubling rate, the correlation Kellogg invokes between the scale of interest rates and the corresponding time needed to double the principal of any loan (the point at which the interest paid out equals the original principal borrowed):

15 percent = 4.8 years
10 percent = 7.2 years
5 percent = 14.4 years

3 percent = 24 years
2 percent = 36 years
1 percent = 72 years

An entire economy which carried a perpetual 15% real debt load, for instance, would have to double in size every 4.8 years to produce enough new goods and services to sustain the rate of repayment required by a 15% rate of interest, without selling assets to do so. What does that mean in real terms? The highest annual U.S. economic growth ever achieved was 19% during World War II, never before or since approached. In recent decades, the annual adjusted economic growth rate of the U.S. economy has been in the range of 3% or so, and gradually declining. Very high interest rates, such as 15%, presume at least a nominal growth rate of similar magnitude. Although Paul Volcker as Federal Reserve head famously spiked interest rates to nearly 20% in 1981, and brought rampant inflation under control, the United States' growth rate at the time was far less.

But how much is too much? Even at a 3% perpetual debt load, all other things being equal, the economy would have to double in size every twenty-four years to meet the production goals determined by that rate. Thus, a $1 million dollar loan from the creditor, if everything goes as all parties imagine, turns into $2 million in twenty-four years. Keep in mind that $1 million of this $2 million is paid off to discharge the principal of the loan, and is thereby extinguished (removed from circulation), while the second $1 million is paid to the lender as interest. The borrower, however, is obligated to pay *both* these charges. He or she is legally required to hand over $2 million of his or her own money over twenty-four years in return for $1 million upfront at the start. The creditor has the borrowers' collateral and the power of the state to enforce contracts as security, not to mention the bankers' access to loans or bailouts from the central bank or the government, if needed.

What would it mean to literally double the economy every twenty-four years as would be required to keep solvent with a 3% ongoing debt burden? By 'economy' we understand the tangible process of extraction, production, distribution, and consumption. What can we see and feel of the economy? How can we measure it? Imagine if every community—yours and mine—became literally twice as big over a twenty-four-year period. That would mean twice as many people consuming twice as many goods and services over that period. On the mile and a half long road where I live in rural upstate New York, for instance, there are currently eight residential structures. A doubled economy, if we understand that to literally mean doubling the entire living stock of a community (or nation), means doubling everything, (people, the housing stock, factories, roads, buildings, stores, appliances, cars, ships, airplanes, etc.). That would yield sixteen houses on my road in twenty-four years, a 100% increase in about one generation. That would be a dramatic, qualitative change. It would transform my neighborhood from rural to suburban in density. Even more dramatically, after ninety-six years of 3% interest, less than a century, I could expect 128 houses on my road, with my suburban neighborhood now transformed into an urban one. And if I left my road after twenty-four years and traveled the nation, I would see the same doubling of everything everywhere. By real comparison, there were seven houses on my road twenty-four years ago, and eight today, for a real world increase over that period of 14%.

Here's Kellogg talking about the doubling rate in the idiom of his day:

> At the age of twenty-one, D. owns a well improved farm of one hundred acres. He leases it to E. at an interest of seven per cent., payable in land, as the interest on money is payable in money. At the close of the year, E. pays D. seven acres of as good quality as the one hundred rented, with a *pro rata* proportion of buildings upon them. D. continues to let the farm to E. requiring him to pay the rent in land half-yearly as interest, as interest on money is paid half-yearly in money; and to pay rent on the land so paid, as the borrower of money pays interest on the interest which he adds half yearly to the principal. In ten years, E. must pay one farm; in twenty years, three farms; in thirty years, seven farms; in forty years, fifteen farms; . . . and in seventy years, one hundred and twenty-seven farms; all in as good a state of cultivation as the one originally leased. At the age of ninety-one, D. can bequeath to his posterity one hundred and twenty seven farms, from the mere rent of one. These farms E. must earn by the labor of seventy years, and pay to D. for the use of one farm. If it were possible for him to earn the one hundred and twenty-seven farms to pay to D., and the rate of interest were reduced to one per cent., he need pay to D. only about one farm as the rent for the seventy years, and would retain one hundred and twenty-six as the surplus of his labor.[22]

Kellogg's measure of the doubling rate of interest illustrates the phenomenon of exponential growth. The dynamic accumulation (the rate of doubling) demanded by the interest on loans arguably has been the main engine driving modern economies.[23] The vast expansion of credit, beginning with the financial revolution after 1700, gave landowners, industrialists, and other entrepreneurs, a greatly enhanced ability to command and develop resources for profit. The principal limiting condition has been the demand that profits keep ahead of the interest payments on the loans financing those profits. It turned out that the abundance and potency of the new resources when put to work by the industrial revolution (particularly fossil fuels) vastly exceeded expectations and allowed for a long run of credit financed economic growth benefiting creditors and debtors alike. When the doubling time of the interest rate exceeds the doubling time of the actual economy, however, we overshoot the carrying capacity of the economy. Although exponential economic growth historically has been able to keep pace with the demands of interest rates for roughly three hundred years, that appears no longer to be the case.[24]

In the aggregate, in a modern economy running on perpetual debt, the economy would have to run on perpetual growth; it would have to grow proportionally with the rate of interest on debt in order for its payments to be absorbed over time in full discharge of the debt. If productivity fails to keep up with lending, we end up with more debt than the economy can absorb. Our dollars become inflated in value, and purchase less and less. At the same time, excess debt destabilizes the economy by increasing bankruptcies and liquidations, which feed asset deflation. This tension, if it gets too great, is released in a market crash, usually a sudden and surprising one, in which debts are liquidated rather than redeemed, and after which the economy can begin once more to reabsorb debt. Call this the business cycle.

Kellogg makes it clear that whether economic growth can sustain the credit it demands or not, the borrowing classes are committed to produce for their creditors as well as for themselves. That's arguably a form of indentured servitude, which ought to be illegal. It's a transfer of wealth which is unearned income for the creditors. At 3% interest, debtors will not only have to build an economy to support themselves over twenty-four years, but at the same time they will have to build a whole new equivalent parallel economy to stand alongside the one which already exists in order to meet the demands of their creditors. The borrower must work overtime, as an indentured servant, even if self-indentured (by signing an agreement to take the loan), to satisfy the demands of a creditor, or master, before he or she can satisfy their own needs. Given their monopoly power, banks and major lenders have been able to charge for loans any amount of interest the loans will bear. This extra interest is an extortion, as populists have argued, a private tax imposed by creditors onto borrowers, authorized solely by virtue of their legalized monopoly power. This is the root social injustice, recognized by Jefferson, analyzed by Kellogg, and decried by later American populists. Instead of maintaining a right to the full fruits of his or her labor, the borrower is forced to share his or her future earnings with the creditor. The much fuller life, which would be possible if the borrower could retain the full surplus of his or her own labor, is sacrificed for no other reason than bankers are able to extort a monopoly price for the credit they control.

Imposing unearned interest charges is a form of rent-seeking, or unearned income, a form of consumption without production. Private bankers charge interest on the presumption that they are the owners of the money which they create by making loans. Yet, as we've seen, at no point can the money be found to be actually in their possession (possession being a necessary attribute of ownership by most measures).[25] It comes into existence only at the point where it comes into the possession of *someone other than the lender*, in this case, the borrower. As we shall see, a public banking system—as proposed by Kellogg and his populist followers—could work the same way as the private banking system. It too could satisfy the financial needs of the community on the basis of modern bank money created through fractional reserve lending, but it would do so as a public service, as a non-profit or for-cost lender to the public. It would demand no unearned interest income in return. Insofar as the borrower is as essential to the creation and regulation of credit-debt money as is the lender, a democratically accountable public banking system would be expected to do justice to the needs of the borrowers.

The bankers, as we've seen, did not openly deny the power of the sovereign over money; they co-opted it instead. Their 'English system' ingeniously masked private money creation and usurious unearned interest charges with the superficial stamp of government approval of bank money as legal tender for all debts, public and private. It was a fateful trade-off, initially made by a weak sovereign to solve its debt problems. Because of this, sovereign power over money in most Western countries—where private bank money has been allowed free rein, beginning with the British financial revolution—has continued to remain weak and mostly symbolic to this day. Modern governments in most Western countries have surrendered money creation and management to the private banking system, and continue to be financially dependent on private wealth, just like William III was. Sovereign states can tax and borrow, but although they can create money, they have delegated that power to the hands of private bankers. The only advantage to the state, which must borrow like anyone else, is that it's usually the largest single borrower not easily ignored. Since it alone has the power of taxation, its financial credibility trumps that of other borrowers, which is what allows it to be used by private bankers as a backstop for their system.

Full public control over money creation and distribution would require the overthrow of 'the English system,' and the complete restoration of the sovereign's monopoly power over money. What would that mean? What kinds of sovereign money are possible? How can public control of money best be achieved? The version of sovereign money explored in the remainder of this work proposes to create credit-debt money through a public banking system, which would serve the public as the private system currently does, but without the onerous interest rates private banks extract. As Kellogg made plain in his analysis, and as we shall see in detail, a public lending system run at cost, not for profit, with a non-usurious rate of interest, is designed to ensure that the borrowing public would retain virtually all the benefits of any loan they took out.

Kellogg's strategy, as adopted by later populists, was not to condemn the new credit money institutionalized by 'the English system,' but to transfer it from private to public ownership and operate it on a non-profit, non-usurious basis for the common good. This was the deepest vision of monetary reform proposed by classic, nineteenth century American populists. They understood and valued property and capitalism as personal rights. They ardently wished to see property and capitalism decentralized and spread throughout society. They argued that the financial abuses which concentrated property in few hands and distorted capitalism stemmed from the privatized pro-profit monopoly over the bank-money system which allowed creditors to exploit debtors. The bank money system itself they wished to preserve for public rather than private benefit. For them, access to property was secured by a right of access to credit.

NOTES

1. Frederick Soddy, *Wealth, Virtual Wealth and Debt* (London: George Allen, reprint 1983), 137–38.

2. For a recent, in-depth history of money and society, see *Money Changes Everything: How Finance Made Civilization Possible*, William N. Goetzmann (Princeton: Princeton University Press, 2017).

3. See Goetzmann, ibid, chapters 1–4. See also Daniel Dematos, "Sumerian Loans," *The Tontine Coffeehouse: A History of Finance*, November 28, 2022, https://tontinecoffeehouse.com/2022/11/28/sumerian-loans/.

4. See David Graeber, *Debt: The First 5,000 Years* (Brooklyn: Melville House, 2011), especially chapters 1–3. See also Michael Hudson,. . . . *and forgive them their debts: Lending, Foreclosure, and Redemption from Bronze Age Finance to the Jubilee Year* (Dresden: Islet-Verlag, 2018); and Michael Hudson and Marc Van de Mieroop, *Debt and Economic Renewal in the Ancient Near East* (Bethesda: CDL, 2002).

5. Graeber, ibid., 40.

6. Hudson, op. cit., *Debt and Economic Renewal*, 31.

7. See Demotas, op. cit.

8. See Leslie Kurke, *Coins, Bodies, Games, and Gold* (Princeton: Princeton University Press, 1999); see also Robert Tye, *Gyges' Magic Ring? The Origins of Coinages and Open Societies* (York: Published by Robert Tye, revised version, 2013, New Preface, 2022), https://www.academia.edu/356701/Gyges_Magic_Ring_The_Origin_of_Coinages_and_Open_Societies_2022_update.

9. See William N. Goetzmann, *Money Changes Everything: How Finance Made Civilization Possible* (Princeton: Princeton University Press, 2017), chapters 5 and 6

10. Ibid., 123.

11. Ibid., 135.

12. Insofar as the development of coinage and finance in India, China, and the East proceeded on relatively independent lines until modern times, the history of Western finance has been largely self-contained until recently.

13. See Sydney Homer and Richard Sylla, *A History of Interest Rates,* 3rd ed. (Rutgers, Rutgers University Press, 1996), et. passim.

14. Cf. Adrian Kuzminski, *The Ecology of Money: Debt, Growth, and Sustainability* (Lanham, MD: Lexington Books, 2013).

15. Scott Nevil, "Fractional Reserve Banking and How It Works," in *Investopedia* (December, 2022), https://www.investopedia.com/terms/f/fractionalreservebanking.asp.

16. But see Nathan Lewis, "The BRICS Go for Gold," *Forbes*, July 16, 2023.

17. Christopher Hollis, *The Two Nations: A Financial Study of English History* (New York: Gordon Press, 1975), 29–30.

18. Alexander Hamilton, "From Alexander Hamilton to James Duane" [September 3, 1780], in *Founders Online* (National Archives, https://founders.archives.gov/documents/Hamilton/01-02-02-0838).

19. Jeremy Bentham, *Defense of Usury* (Liberty Fund: Library of Liberty [1787]), https://oll.libertyfund.org/title/bentham-defence-of-usury.

20. Edward Kellogg, *A New Monetary System* (New York: Bert Franklin, 1970 [1861]), 80.

21. Ibid., 81.

22. Ibid., 83–84.

23. See Adrian Kuzminski, *The Ecology of Money: Debt Growth and Sustainability* (Lanham, MD: Lexington Books, 2013), chapter 5, "The Industrial Revolution."

24. See Chris Martenson, *The Crash Course: The Unsustainable Future of Our Economy, Energy, and Environment* (Hoboken: John Wiley & Sons, 2011), et passim; see also Donella Meadows, et al., *Limits to Growth: The 30-Year Update* (White River Junction: Chelsea Green, 2004), et passim; see also William R. Catton, Jr., *Overshoot: The Ecological Basis of Revolutionary Change* (Urbana: University of Illinois Press, 1982), et passim.

25. See Richard A. Werner, "Can Banks Individually Create Money Out of Nothing?—The Theories and the Empirical Evidence" *International Review of Financial Analysis* 36 (2014): 1–19.

Chapter 3

Democratic Capitalism

American populism and its revolutionary monetary proposals are steeped in American history. Questions about property, credit, and interest came to America defined by struggles in the Old World. The question of debt had been chronic in European history, ancient and modern, with debt often blamed as the chief instrument promoting economic and social inequalities common across the Old World. Inequality was what most people experienced and took for granted. Exceptions—such egalitarian communities as existed—were small, archaic, and isolated. A fair distribution of wealth could only be imagined abstractly by most Europeans, who had little if any direct experience of it. In the long course of European history there was little escape from the tensions between already established social orders over the distribution of wealth—tensions between monarchs and subjects, citizens and slaves, lords and peasants, capitalists and workers, and men and women, among others. The question of debt cut across and reinforced all of these inequalities.

America was different. North America in particular provided relatively open access to resources by ordinary people upon arrival not available, or even imaginable, to them in Europe. Once its indigenous peoples had been tragically ravaged by disease in the wake of initial European contact, and the remainder conquered and marginalized by the occupying European colonists, the continent stood open to new settlers for the basic effort of claiming its lands and appropriating its productive capacity. Free immigrants were able to appropriate for themselves resources largely available for the taking in an open continent, something not possible in Europe, and hardly anywhere else (Australia comes to mind). It is here, with this new access to capital, that we find the core American identity with personal freedom.

This unique American experience didn't make America wholly exceptional. Far from it. The Euro-Americans brought with them all the evils and vices of the Old World, including the intolerances bred by religion, greed, patriarchy, paternalism, racism, and slavery. Some of these, particularly slavery, they deepened for the worst. In our time the full depth of these evils is being more widely probed than ever before, and American history is being reevaluated accordingly. What nonetheless remained exceptional in America was the situation created by largely free access to resources of open land on the frontier to those who were free and able enough to get there. These exceptional circumstances appeared first in the Americas, at least in modern history, but once understood the freedoms they enabled are arguably applicable anywhere. What concerns us here is the significance such a state of affairs holds for anyone able to benefit from it, and what it can mean as a precedent for reforming our own troubled affairs. The frontier allowed ordinary citizens, then mainly free white males and their families, who would have been propertyless in Europe (or Asia, or Africa), to acquire land in America. They had the opportunity to command resources and become independent producers—farmers, artisans, mechanics, teamsters, builders, merchants, shopkeepers, lawyers, doctors, among many other small business entrepreneurs—and they forged in the process a unique sensibility found among Americans, a love of self-sufficient freedom, shared by very many if not all Americans, an identity of independent proprietorship epitomized by the farmer and small business owner.

Frederick Jackson Turner famously derived this uniquely American identity from the role of the frontier in American life.[1] The frontier offered accessibility to property and resources which in turn created an expanded middle class of citizens who were free because they themselves owned and operated the means of production. They could compete or cooperate, but they were above all independent players in a common economic game of human-scale capitalism. They hired employees as needed, but not on an industrial scale. They were not compelled to work for anyone else, but only for themselves and their families. They were not proletarians; they were business owners; and in their day, they (and their households) made up the vast majority of Americans.

Theirs was not the pseudo-exceptionalism of twentieth-century American global-empire building, but a real exceptionalism first manifest in early America—a decentralized democratic society marked by widespread private ownership of property. This was the Jeffersonian tradition early on symbolized by the yeoman farmer and the town meeting; it linked political independence and citizenship to the ownership of property. This was a world, to be sure, from which most people were formally excluded from decision making (including women, slaves, and native peoples), but the rights and responsibilities initially secured for property owning white males turned out to be values to which nearly everyone (including women, slaves, and native peoples) could aspire because they were the values of free citizens. The free citizen is a person of minimal property, perhaps, yet enough of a property owner so as to be insulated from abject dependence upon his or her economic betters. The independent ownership of property, and the responsibilities and security it entailed, gave property owning citizens an independent political voice not easily silenced or fooled. The populist aim was to extend the right to private property, to some fair measure of capital resources, to all. The right to property is not just the right to work, but the right to have something to work with, to have access to productive resources, to materials, to money, to capital, to ownership.

The introduction of socialist ideas from Europe, into which fit preexisting norms of chronic class struggle, obscured this American exceptionalism that socialists have never understood. European-inspired socialists presumed that the power of capitalism would inevitably be as concentrated as the power of feudalism had been. Just as there had been lords and peasants, so there would be capitalists and workers. American exceptionalism—forged most sharply on the Western frontier, and perhaps best memorialized in countless Western films—rejected these Old World hierarchies. It represented something new: a personalized capitalism which was decentralized and democratized, not impersonally centralized and monopolized. Above all, it was presumed to be accessible to all. Fundamental to this capitalism was the presumption of a universal right to property. This populist capitalist sensibility—based on property and assets widely distributed among roughly egalitarian citizens, making them all more or less capitalists—was a vision otherwise unprecedented in modern history.

The right to property or assets was embodied above all in land, and also in gold and silver and other assets, but for practical and general purposes, it is at bottom a right to credit, to money, which is the gateway to access real property. Even small business is usually impossible to conduct without extending credit, borrowing money, and assuming other forms of debt. Credit provides immediate access to capital (borrowed money), available on the moral and legal condition of a debt obligation of repayment. Fair and uniform standards of access to credit, as in a public banking system run on an at-cost basis as a public service (not as a private for-profit business), aim to ensure, as we shall see below and in chapter 5, that the benefits of the money created for the borrower remain with the borrower, not the lender.

This populist democratic capitalism was articulated most clearly in movements defending democracy, property, and self-rule in colonial and ante-bellum America, and it remained a central force in American life down to the 1890s, when the populists finally lost their long war against bankers and creditors. Populism—the dual demand for democracy *and* property, for what might be called 'democratic capitalism'—is arguably the fundamental American identity. The link between property and democracy—already evident in ancient and medieval city states—may not be unique to American populists, but they gave it one of its last and deepest expressions. They also attempted to extend its application beyond local communities to the larger nation as a whole. The classic populists aspired to a norm of widely distributed ownership of resources made possible by monetary reform through public banking, thereby securing the relative economic and political independence of individuals and households. The exceptionalism embedded in classical American populism is distinguished by its understanding that the relative *economic* independence of citizens is a necessary condition of their ability to participate freely and honestly in democratic decision making. The defeat of the populists was coincidental with the rise of mass factory wage-labor in place of dispersed self-employment and small business proprietorships. The loss of economic independence by wage-earners was cushioned for a time by the labor movement, and by liberal and progressive reformers, until it too fell before the renewed late-twentieth-century corporate onslaught of deregulation and labor outsourcing.[2]

***

The populists may have embodied American exceptionalism, but they had to contend with the monopolists who came to control major economic choke points, demanded monopoly prices for the products and the services they provided, and threatened to seize control of the economy. The railroads were the most conspicuous early industrial monopoly. Farmers especially in the south and west had little choice but to ship their grain via rail at exorbitant rates, and they bitterly complained. Monopolies emerged in the robber baron era after the Civil War in heavy industries such as steel and energy (coal and oil), transportation (railroads), communications (telegraph), chemicals, mining, and agriculture (tobacco, sugar).

But perhaps the most compelling monopoly, the one which affected nearly all producers, was the private banking monopoly controlling lending and interest rates. Private bankers make their fortunes, as we have seen, by charging rates of interest which ensure a steady transfer of a large portion of the earnings of borrowers into the hands of the bankers. It was the populists above all who challenged this monopoly power of the banks by questioning what they saw as usurious and unjust rates of interest undermining the right to property.

Today, interest rates are taken for granted and seldom questioned. The populists were perhaps the last major social movement to question their existence. Why do we need interest rates at all? Why can't we have credit without interest? Is there a just or natural rate of interest? When does interest become usurious? Credit, we should remind ourselves, is necessary to any functioning economy. Since it can be invented out of nothing, as we now know, its creation cost is zero. As the principal is repaid, the money borrowed and spent into the economy is taken back out of it, and extinguished. The goods and resources consumed in the process, however, remain to be replenished. They constitute our liabilities to the environment.

One way to compensate for our consumption would be to pay a rate of interest equal to the rate of consumption, that is, to the rate of depreciation of the resources enabled by the loan. A natural interest rate, on that basis, would be the surplus which must be produced, at a minimum, to replenish such resources as are needed in order to keep the economy at a steady state of economic activity. A perpetual rate of zero-interest loans will not do. It would require borrowers to produce only enough to extinguish the money they borrowed. It would do nothing towards replenishing the resources they have consumed in spending down the money they borrowed. In a zero-interest economy there would be little if any incentive for private holders of money to lend, and, most importantly, no incentive at all for borrowers from any source, public or private, to replenish any of the resources which the money they borrowed allowed them to consume.

Otherwise, if the borrower must pay some rate of interest, they (or someone on their behalf) is obligated to produce a surplus of production in proportion to the rate of interest they are charged. That surplus is what allows the borrower to pay the interest. This is how interest drives economic development—at least as long as there are willing borrowers. But what rate of interest will match the needed rate of replenishment? Can a just rate of interest, one which falls short of being usurious, be determined? Unfortunately, as we've seen, critics of usurious lending have failed to establish what that rate would be.

The benchmark for determining a natural, non-usurious rate of interest is what it takes to maintain a steady-state, self-replicating economy. In such an economy, borrowers paying interest would, at a minimum, need to produce only enough extra products and services to generate enough capital for the next generation of borrowers to be able to produce and consume at the same level. Such a steady state of production would provide for the continuous replenishment of goods and services as they are depreciated or consumed. The individual portion we as individuals owe to that ongoing replenishment is the sum of what we ourselves consume and wear out over the course of our own lifetimes: our homes, our vehicles, our foods, our clothes, our roads, our farms, our factories, our energy, that is, virtually everything we use which must be replenished. To merely tread-water economically we need to pay not only for what we consume *but for the cost of replacing it*. The minimum rate of steady state economic activity can be understood as the natural replacement rate required by economic entropy, that is, by the depreciation of the resources (materials and labor, goods and services) for which we must somehow compensate to maintain our very existence.

It is an intriguing, and perhaps auspicious, coincidence that the time required for 1% interest to equal the principle in payment, or seventy-two years, approximates a traditional adult human lifetime. The interest charged on loans—the amount necessary to reinvest to keep a steady state economy going—would naturally come out at about 1% *if we took our own average lifetimes as the measure of replenishment*. Fixing interest rates at 1% would ensure that borrowers would have to maintain a minimal 1% surplus of their production over a lifetime to replenish their share of consumption, while at the same time freeing them of any further, or usurious, debt burden. With new borrowers continuously replacing old borrowers, the ecological 1% rate on loans becomes perpetual. The principal would be extinguished as it was repaid, like all successful loans, but the accrued 1% interest would automatically guarantee that the resources consumed would be steadily replenished. Usury, then, can be defined following Kellogg, as any interest rate in excess of 1%.

If the idea of a fixed, 1% rate of interest may seem fanciful to the reader, consider "In Defense of Low Interest Rates" by James K. Galbraith, which challenges the presumption of large and variable rates as a normal, inevitable, socially useful financial mechanism. Although interest rates have been understood historically as a natural reflection of risk which sets the price point for the capital markets, Galbraith rejects this argument, which he says is "is wholly circular; it assumes the existence of a natural rate and of market forces that cause actual rates to fluctuate around it."[3] As American productive activity shifted offshore after the 1980s, especially to China, low rates at home (backed by U.S. Treasuries as the principal world asset) continued to encourage investment. But the lack of productive domestic opportunity meant that money went into speculation instead, mainly into real estate. Galbraith invokes John Maynard Keynes, for whom "interest was the return to the provider of funds, typically the idle *rentier*. Thus a low rate of interest and a high rate of investment would yield, in the long term, a 'euthanasia of the rentier'—leaving capitalist society in the hands of its active elements, namely businesses, their workers, consumers, and the government."[4] Low interest credit is essential to economic production, and high, unearned or speculative or usurious rates are economically injurious, and accrue only to *rentiers*, that is, creditors.

For Kellogg, the stability of the dollar, or any currency, can be guaranteed only if it is lent out at a fixed rate of interest established by law and backed by productive assets. If the cost of running a steady-state economy can be understood as the rate of entropy calculated by the human consumption of resources over a lifetime, then the interest rate appropriate to maintaining steady-state consumption turns out to be the same as the 1% per year rate Kellogg determined should be the fixed rate on all public credit loans. In paying back 1% on their loans, the borrowing public would not only be replenishing the principal but also guaranteeing to society that their use of their loans will not deplete our common pool of resources. This does not mean that the economy itself is limited to a no-growth, steady-state. That depends on the available resources. But it does mean that borrowers will be free of usurious rates, and that the benefits of those savings will be theirs to invest instead for themselves as they see fit.

***

The vision of a public banking system loaning money at a 1% rate of interest, underwriting a broad economy of democratic capitalism, was the deepest vision produced by classic nineteenth century American populist thinkers. It was developed most fully by Edward Kellogg, who proposed establishing a nation-wide system of public credit he called the National Safety Fund. Kellogg was an antebellum businessman in New York City who suffered the crash of 1837 and became a writer and popular advocate of monetary reform. His main works, noted in the introduction, are *Labor and Other Capital* (1849), and a revised version, *A New Monetary System* (1861), posthumously edited by his daughter, Mary Kellogg Putnam.

Populists like Kellogg were squarely in the Jeffersonian tradition. They were distrustful of monopolies—of concentrations of power either in big business or big government. They either opposed private banking, including the privately owned First and Second National Banks, in favor of free banking, or, like Kellogg, they proposed a public banking system in its place. Some early populists, like the New York editorialist William Leggitt, supported market-dependent free private banking, with little or no state regulation.[5] Kellogg and many later populists, however, had no confidence in private banking, especially free banking. They saw the lack of interoperability among thousands of local, independent banks whose notes, lacking adequate coordination or a uniform standard of issue, were variable and unstable in value. More fundamentally, the for-profit private basis of free private banking, like any private banking, usurped what Kellogg and later populists came to regard as an essential public function. An interoperable banking system—having to be totally fluid and one and the same for all—made banking into a natural property of everyone, the financial commons, and a natural public monopoly.

Kellogg proposed to replace the private banking monopoly over money with what he called the National Safety Fund—a decentralized system of public banking, the first of its kind to be proposed. Previously, nearly all banks, even the biggest ones, were private banks; public banking was rare to nonexistent for most people. Temples and shrines had provided safekeeping for money in antiquity; as religious and charitable institutions and monastic orders did in medieval Europe. Feudal municipal corporations also held money, and sometimes provided loans to the public on collateral. Venice experimented with a public bank after the collapse of its private banks in the sixteenth century. But the only major exception to private banking in the premodern period was the Bank of Amsterdam, active in the seventeenth and eighteenth centuries. It was the public bank of the city of Amsterdam, and its commissioners were elected by the city council. The bank offered accounts for individuals, who were given certificates for their deposits of coin and precious metals. These certificates circulated widely among third parties to settle exchanges and pay off debts, becoming a *de facto* currency. The Bank of Amsterdam did not, however, practice the kind of fractional reserve banking invented by the goldsmiths. Like the bank of Venice before it, it insisted on 100% reserves for its loans, which were made mainly for government projects and large commercial ventures. It did *not* create credit-money, in contrast to the goldsmiths and their successors, who perfected 'the English system.' The Bank of Amsterdam's credit remained limited by the amount of real money on deposit. It did not expand the money supply.

Kellogg proposed something different in the way of public banking, something revolutionary: a decentralized public banking system which created money by lending to individuals on a fractional reserve basis, just as private bankers were doing, but on a non-usurious, cost basis as a public benefit. Like the populists generally, Kellogg understood and feared the power of private credit money; but at the same time he appreciated its benefits, especially the broader access to credit it made possible. The idea of replacing a private monopoly power of fractional reserve money creation with a public monopoly power of fractional reserve money creation would be of no benefit, however, unless the abuses of the former were eliminated while its benefits were retained.

A non-usurious fixed rate of interest rate at 1% should be understood as the interest rate justified by nature insofar as it would compel the borrowing public to produce in their lifetimes only as much as is necessary to replenish the resources they consume in the ordinary course of events. According to Kellogg, as an obligation to future generations in order to ensure our survival as a species and to replenish what we consume, we are socially justified and morally obligated to pay an interest rate of 1% to ensure that end. He meant that the interest rate would be fixed by law to a perpetual 1%. It would be illegal to borrow money at any higher rate. Any production beyond the obligation to maintain a steady state or status quo society is production rightfully belonging to the producers, to those actually carrying out that production, not to their creditors. Any rate above 1% compels the appropriation of resources beyond that of a steady state economy and transfers their value from borrowers to creditors. It forces the economy to depart from a steady state and enter a growth state, even at the cost of depleting resources and concentrating wealth. A 1% rate, on the other hand, does not preclude growth any more than it commands it. Any growth which loans at 1% are able to stimulate will be entirely in response to the economic conditions and resources and opportunities available. The maximal benefits of debt will remain the assets of the borrowers, not the creditors.

The principal abuse of private banking in Kellogg's understanding was not fractional reserve money creation itself, but the free-floating and potentially unlimited rates of interest charged by private bankers at the expense of their borrowers. Usury—an unjust extortion of wealth—was their crime. Kellogg is aware, and discusses at length, what we call fractional reserve banking, and he makes no complaint against it as such. His concern is rather to establish the viability of paper money issued as credit to borrowers apart from any need for a reserve in commodity money, or specie, to redeem the paper notes. The true reserve for paper money notes, he argues, is the land or such other sufficient productive collateral which can secure the backing for the issuance of such notes in the first place. "The people furnish the security for the bank-notes," Kellogg points out, "and pay the interest, which is the source of all the gains of the banks."[6] The true basis of fractional reserve lending is not traditional cash bank reserves—which nonetheless remain necessary to cover withdrawals—but the value of the collateral put up by borrowers to secure the loans in the first place.

***

The populists were part of a broader social and political world in which their fate was played out. The decades after the Civil War witnessed a sharp rise of discontent among both urban industrial workers and farmers across large parts of the country. The war had stimulated the economy to unprecedented levels of growth. As the economy boomed, farmers and small businesspeople took out loans on the prospect of continuing expansion. But overproduction and new connections to world markets, made possible by the buildout of railroads, combined to lower prices, especially in agriculture, still the bellwether of the national economy. The debt burden for many turned into a debt nightmare. The struggle over money and credit in America, came to a climax after the market crash of 1893, with creditors willing and able to reassert their authority over debtors (through liens, foreclosures, tax sales, and other legal instruments).[7] Failing to obtain political and financial relief they desperately needed, the populist movements found themselves politically isolated and pushed to the sidelines; they and their ideas have been shut out from public debate ever since. To understand this setback to the most powerful movement ever to restore sovereign control over money in the United States, a look back at the history of this critical period will be useful.

The unprecedented economic boom after the Civil War was stimulated in large part by the issuance of Greenbacks by the federal government to fund the war effort. Greenbacks were unbacked fiat money, issued by the Treasury Department in payment for services rendered to the government. Earlier fiat money precedents include the scripts issued by colonial governments, beginning with Massachusetts in 1690, the Continentals issued during the Revolutionary War, and the *assignants* of the French Revolution, among others. Most of these currencies were intended to meet government expenses in stressful circumstances, usually war, where hard money (specie) was scarce. Once issued, unbacked fiat currencies proved hard to take out of circulation, even if accepted for taxes, with serious inflation often following in their wake. Greenbacks were a revival of a native American tradition of unbacked fiat money. Once put into circulation to pay war contractors, Greenbacks flowed into the general economy to fuel investment and production. Although any state sanctioned currency—even gold—can be considered a fiat currency simply by virtue of that sanction, a pure or unbacked fiat currency (not redeemable by anything at all) has *only* its state sanction to back it up.

Greenbacks were more successful than most fiat currencies. About $450 million in notes were issued and remained in circulation from 1862 to 1879. The Lincoln administration resorted to fiat money only after balking at the rates private Wall Street bankers proposed to charge for war loans to the government. The bankers kept up a steady resistance to the new currency, calling for a retirement of the notes and a return to specie and to the private banks' monopoly over money creation. Farmers and other producers, appreciating the new easy money, fought to retain and expand the new currency. The crash of 1873 brought these issues to the fore. Greenbacks had suffered from volatility against specie, rising as high as 25:1 against gold, with inflation rates soaring to near 25%, though they recovered some of their value after the war. Nonetheless, as with any large and sudden issuance of currency, they initially strongly stimulated the economy. The resulting inflation offered debtors some relief at the expense of creditors, which encouraged them to take on more debt to expand with the economy. Most producers, especially farmers, benefited from the higher prices. But at the same time Greenbacks concentrated wealth into the hands of government contractors, who were the first users of the new money. Much of this concentrated wealth found its way into Wall Street speculation, culminating in the 1873 crash.

The bankers, never happy about Greenbacks, pushed back and persuaded Congress to pass the Resumption Act, by which Greenbacks were redeemed and phased out at the end of 1879. The fiat money experiment, and the state sovereignty over money it reintroduced, was over for the time being, but fiat money advocates fought on. The Greenbackers formed their own political party and sought to reinstate the Greenbacks, or some version of fiat money. They are the direct ancestors of today's progressive monetary reformers. Failing to reestablish fiat money, many Greenbackers reverted to support for commodity money, especially silver, in the belief that sufficient silver supplies existed, especially in western states, to mine and mint and expand the money supply.

***

Kellogg clearly distinguished himself from both these schools early on. In his 1841 *A Treatise on the Currency and the Exchanges*, he wrote, "Taking therefore a general ground, I reject those views held by one part of the community, viz.: that it is not the duty of Government to regulate the exchanges, and maintain a sound currency; but that these things be left to take care of themselves. . . . Neither am I prepared to adopt those views advocated by others, that the General Government has the power, and it is its duty, not only to maintain a sound currency and regulate the exchanges, but to create a currency and supply the means of commerce by chartering a National Bank of circulation, discount, and deposit."[8]

Kellogg, in short, rejects both commodity money and fiat money theories. He goes on to outline instead a middle path, or third way, between these extremes. He proceeds deductively, in rational enlightenment fashion, from first principles, as follows: "Government is an institution ordained by the Supreme Being. It is the *agent* employed by society to protect its interest and promote its welfare. Its first great end is the protection of life . . . the second is the protection of property."[9] Kellogg's concern is with the failure of government to protect property by its failure to 'regulate the exchanges,' as he puts it, by which he means the commercial credit markets. Business dependence on the private banks' monopoly over money creation through lending at interest left borrowers vulnerable to arbitrary changes in the interest rates, and therefore in the value of money, leading to inflationary booms and deflationary busts—the familiar financial cycle of speculation, growth, panic, and collapse.

Neither commodity nor fiat money can address this problem for Kellogg. He proposes another alternative, a new innovative plan:

> Which is, that Congress shall establish a National Institution, which shall have power to make collections of notes and drafts, negotiate bills of exchange among the various states, and in general to conduct the exchange operations of the country. Its exclusive employment shall be that of providing a sound, legitimate, uniform, and convenient currency throughout the United States, and regulating

> domestic exchanges; and in being the Fiscal Agent of the Government, it shall also collect, keep, and disburse the public revenue, as Congress or the Treasury Department shall direct. This Institution shall be prohibited from discounting notes and drafts, or loaning money, and also from receiving money on deposit except Government funds. And all State and private Banks, and corporate companies of circulation, discount, and deposit, shall be prohibited from dealing in exchange, and shall be confined to circulation, discount, and deposit.[10]

Kellogg makes a sharp distinction, carried through in his later work, between state and private institutions engaged in lending and money creation, of which he disapproves, and a national agency guaranteeing a sound currency for the nation, which he recommends. Kellogg doesn't yet say here how the national Institution will 'conduct the exchange operations of the country,' and guarantee the currency, but in his mature works he proposes it will do so by fixing a low rate of interest on loans (the 1% at which he ultimately arrived). This means that the creation of money and its use in exchange will no longer be distorted by arbitrary rates set by money lenders. Nonetheless, and crucially, the creation of money (paper currency, or notes) remains in the hands, not of the National Institution, but of local public banks—the branches of the National Institution—which retain the power of lending to the public (circulation, discount, and deposit) denied the National Institution itself.

At this stage, in *A Treatise on the Currency and the Exchanges*, Kellogg still presumes money creation to be the private banking function it was in his day (and still remains). But later, as we shall see in the last chapter, Kellogg reached the logical conclusion that non-usurious local money creation on what amounts to a non-profit basis is best conducted by the government as a natural monopoly through local public banks. In the final version of his decentralized system, however, he maintains and finalizes the sharp and fundamental distinction between a non-lending, non-money creating National Institution dedicated solely to the regulation of the currency by a fixed rate of interest, and the local creation of money through lending.

***

Unfortunately, Kellogg's monetary ideas were reinterpreted after the Civil War in misleading Greenbacker terms and confused with fiat money theories. The key figure in this confusion was Alexander Campbell, author of an influential work published in 1864 whose full title is *The True American System of Finance; the Rights of Labor and Capital, and the Common Sense Way of Doing Justice to the Soldiers and their Families; No Banks: Greenbacks the Exclusive Currency*.[11] Campbell quotes Kellogg's mature work extensively on the nature of money and interest, and in a footnote adds that he was "greatly assisted" by Kellogg's book, *A New Monetary Theory*, which he had procured "after a considerable portion of this pamphlet was written."

It is not clear how well Campbell digested Kellogg's work, especially since most of his own pamphlet had already been drafted. He clearly absorbed two important principles in Kellogg's work: a return to full sovereign control of money, and the ruinous effect of usurious interest rates. But he rejected Kellogg's more fundamental insistence on the issuance of sovereign money by local public banks as loans to individuals. He also watered-down Kellogg's insistence on a just rate of interest at 1%. Campbell's "American system of finance" instead proposed the "issuance of Treasury notes," which he identified as Greenbacks, as legal tender by the federal government in payment for goods and services, along with an issuance of 3% bonds, into which Treasury notes could be converted.

Campbell, writing under the exigencies of a terrible war, proposed a fiat currency, really a defense of the Greenback, whose notes and bonds were to be backed only by the authority of the government. He also permitted a level of usury Kellogg rejected by allowing 3% interest on government bonds. Kellogg's vision of a sovereign debt-money issued by a decentralized public banking system was replaced by Campbell with a vision of a sovereign fiat money centrally issued by the Treasury department. Campbell turned Kellogg inside out, substituting a centrally issued government fiat currency for a decentrally issued government debt-currency.

The misleading assumptions behind Campbell's widely read fiat money proposal worked their way into various anti-monopoly movements, such as the Grange and the Farmers Alliance, which represented coalitions of mostly rural farmers.[12] Most of these movements initially supported the Greenback party founded in 1876. The party elected over twenty Congressman in the late 1870s—a number which would be shocking today—and, in addition to its support of a national fiat currency, it endorsed the eight-hour day, the vote for women, and a universal basic income. The new party was unable, however, to forge an effective alliance with the nascent urban labor movement; it also failed to overcome persistent sectional loyalties to the Republican and Democratic parties, whose leaderships continued to represent the interest of bankers and other monopolists in support of the gold standard, usurious rates of interest, and the private creation of debt-money.

In the face of these political setbacks, including the phasing-out of Greenbacks, the remaining anti-monopolist populists cast about for a new approach. The Farmers Alliance in particular set about building cooperatives among its members as alternative outlets for their products. Alliance members in Texas and the midwest built collective warehouses designed to avoid the onerous burdens imposed by financial middlemen, particularly through the crop-lien system by which landless farmers, or share-croppers, had little choice but to mortgage their crops to pay the rent on their farms. By bringing together their individual crops in central warehouses, farmers hoped to get a better price for farmers by direct sales to distributors, and thus bypass the crop-lien system.

Unfortunately, the cooperative movement failed to raise the money needed to fully fund its cooperative infrastructure. Private bankers, the only real source of adequate capital, refused loans to support an endeavor designed to bypass their business. The failure in 1889 of the largest cooperative venture of the Alliance—the Texas Exchange—prompted a heightened interest in monetary issues, including renewed calls for Greenbacks. At a convention of the Alliance in St. Louis later that year, the most original populist monetary thinker since Kellogg, Charles Macune, proposed something new: a far-reaching alternative to the Greenbackism popular among anti-monopolists, which he called the sub-treasury system.

Macune's sub-treasury system was built on the monetary foundations laid by Kellogg, not the Greenbackers. In direct opposition to the proposals of Greenbackers and Alexander Cambell to create money by government fiat, Macune's sub-treasury system was based on the creation of money as debt in the form of credit advanced to farmers on the security of their products, to be safely stored in regional warehouses under the control of the federal government. Macune followed Kellogg's insight that *a sound sovereign currency could be created by what was in effect a public bank issuing loans to producers with good collateral without imposing usurious interest rates*. Money issued as debt is necessarily tied to production, and thus in principle can be extinguished through debt repayment, as we have argued, more or less in proportion to its creation through lending. Macune's system was described by the classic historian of American populism, Lawrence Goodwyn, as follows:

> Macune's plan called for federal warehouses to be erected in every county in the nation that annually yielded over $500,000 worth of agricultural produce. In these 'sub-treasuries,' farmers could store their crops to await higher prices before selling. They were to be permitted to borrow up to 80 percent of the local market price upon storage, and could sell their sub-treasury 'certificates of deposit' at the prevailing market price at any time of year. Farmers were to pay interest at the rate of 2 per cent per annum, plus small charges for grading, storage, and insurance. Wheat, corn, oats, barley, rye, rice, tobacco, cotton, wool, and sugar were included under the marketing program.[13]

Here we see replicated what is essentially Kellogg's model of public banking: Money is created by a decentralized institution (the federal warehouses, akin to the local Branches of Kellogg's Safety Fund, creating money, 'certificates of deposit,' as debt for producers, albeit at a rate of 2%, in contrast to Kellogg's 1%. Macune's 'certificates of deposit' were backed by the actual production of farmers, much as the dollars issued by the Branches of Kellogg's Safety Fund were backed by the land the farmers put up for collateral. Whereas the currency of Greenbackers and other fiat money advocates has by definition no specific backing, apart from a subjective confidence in the government issuing a currency with no clear standard of redemption, apart from taxes, the collateral to be put up by farmers in the sub-treasuries by contrast would serve as an unequivocal standard of redemption for their 'certificates of deposit.'

***

Macune developed his sub-treasury plan as a leader of the Texas Alliance, subsequently known as the Southern Alliance, the largest of the various Farmers' Alliances. At the December 1889 convention in St. Louis aimed at uniting the Southern and Northern Alliances, Macune formally presented his subtreasury plan for the first time, in effect shifting the key monetary debate from fiat money such as Greenbacks to credit-debt money backed by collateral. Populist historian John D. Hicks describes the scene:

> [T]he introduction of the subtreasury plan aroused 'an animated discussion,' after which it 'was adopted by a large majority.' Following the convention the men responsible for the measure set about to popularize it. Macune in the *National Economist* devoted columns and pages to expounding it and proclaiming its virtues. Polk in *The Progressive Farmer* was not far behind him; nor were the editors of the Southern Alliance papers. Lectures also devoted themselves to the subject; and numerous state Alliance meetings were induced to endorse the plan in terms of glowing commendation. The idea attracted the attention of editorial writers the country over, and while outside Alliance circles the criticism was caustic, the advertising the plan received was thereby enormous.[14]

Macune had moved to Washington to become editor of the *National Economist*, the national voice of the Southern Alliance. The Southern Alliance at its peak claimed a membership of over three million, with thousands of local branches; that, coupled with the large memberships of other Alliances in the North and Midwest, represented a vast grassroots challenge to the emerging, banker dominated system of corporate power now centered in New York and other Eastern cities.

The populist movement led by the Alliance early on had concentrated on its internal organization, developing what we would call today a broad social network, marked by local branches, newspapers, pamphlets, and traveling lecturers. The main focus of the Alliance had been to organize farmers into cooperatives in hopes that sheer numbers and unprecedented coordination would secure control over production and prices. It was all a question of scale. With the failure of the largest cooperative—the Texas Exchange in Dallas—in 1889, these hopes were dashed. The populists, however, doubled down in reaction, now motivated by the new sub-treasury plan. They realized that the fundamental changes they demanded in the nature of money and credit, as well as a number of other issues, could be realized only by gaining national political power and putting their reforms into law.

This effort culminated in the formation of the People's Party in February 1892. The Greenback party had pioneered populist electoral politics, and after its demise the Alliance continued to support individual monetary reform candidates for office, mostly Democrats, with increasing success. In the 1890 elections, the Alliance backed dozens of successful candidates for Congress, often in increasingly uneasy cooperation with the Democratic party. The sub-treasury plan emerged as a controversial issue, resisted by many establishment Democrats as well as nearly all Republicans. The Alliance, under Macune's leadership, decided to stake everything on the sub-treasury plan by forming a third party, the Peoples' Party, with the plan as its financial centerpiece. It was endorsed in the new party's Omaha Platform, adopted at the founding convention in July 1892.[15] The populists would take their vision directly to the people.

The sub-treasury plan found perhaps its purest expression in H. R. 7162, a remarkable bill drafted by Farmers' Alliance leaders and introduced in the House of Representatives in 1890 by John A. Pickler of South Dakota, and in the Senate by Zebulon Vance of North Carolina, titled "A bill to establish a system of sub-treasuries, and for other purposes," which proposed nothing less than the sovereign issuance of credit-debt dollars (denominated in United States treasury notes) by publicly elected county-level sub-treasuries to farmers for 80% of the market value of cotton, wheat oats, corn, and tobacco deposited in the sub-treasuries. The notes were to be "full legal tender for all debts, public and private," and to be counted as "lawful reserve" by banks. They would be lent out at Kellogg's 1% rate of interest. Money repaid for the principal would be extinguished, and the borrower upon redemption of his debt would receive in return the crops originally deposited, or their equivalent, at current market prices.[16] Here was the germ of Kellogg's monetary system potentially applied to the entire American economy. If we imagine extending sub-treasuries into general purpose public banks, and farmers as one group of producers among the general public of diverse producers, it becomes possible to envision any citizen obtaining money at 1% interest on the basis of good collateral. It would not be necessary to physically take the collateral to the public bank, as farmers pledged to take their crops to government warehouses, only to pledge it as a legal liability. Access to credit would be assured as a right for the first time in history. The populists were on a roll.

The Pickler-Vance bill was referred to the Ways and Means Committee in the House and to the Agricultural Committee in the Senate. Hearings were held where Macune and other populist leaders testified, and, in spite of "petitions and memorials, literally by the hundreds,"[17] neither committee took a vote. The results in the 1892 election were impressive, but inconclusive, reflecting a sense of broader public indecision about populist proposals. The Peoples' party nominated a former Greenbacker, James B. Weaver of Iowa, for president, and a former Confederate officer, James G. Field of Virginia, as vice president. The strategy was to build a coalition of southern farmers, ex-Greenbackers, anti-monopolists, northern labor unions, and other reform groups, such as Edward Bellamy's nationalist clubs. The Alliance had supported the 1886 railway strike called by the Knights of Labor and expected their support in turn for the People's Party. In the end, Weaver received over a million popular votes and twenty-two electoral votes, all from Western states. The party won eleven House seats, three Senate seats, and a number of state governorships, results which would be considered revolutionary today.

***

But it was not enough. Outside of some Western states, the party fared poorly. After the election, it split over whether or not the Omaha Platform with the sub-treasury system was an asset or a liability. The so-called 'mid-roaders' supported the platform and the sub-treasury system, eschewing the pro-banking corporatism of both the Democrats and Republicans, while the 'fusionists' rejected the platform, and particularly the sub-treasury plan, and called for integration, mainly with the Democratic party, in last ditch hopes of modifying corporate excesses. The sub-treasury plan for increasing the money supply found itself in competition with new calls for increasing the money supply by the free coinage of silver, which further split the movement.

When the party met at its 1896 convention, on the heels of the Democrats' surprising nomination of William Jennings Bryan for president, along with pro-banking Arthur Sewall for vice president, it voted to endorse Bryan, but nominated its own vice presidential candidate, Tom Watson. This confusing compromise proved fatal. The Republican nominee, William McKinley, handily defeated Bryan and what he called the 'radicals' in the general election, a disaster from which the populist movement never recovered. The bankers and their corporate allies won a decisive victory. They turned back the last serious political challenge they have had to face. The 1892 election turned out to be the highpoint of the populist movement in America.

In the decades after the pivotal 1896 election, the high-minded populism of the Farmers' Alliance descended into the bitter, low-minded politics of resentment, often exploited by demagogues, which has plagued the reputation of populism ever since. The list of latter-day rabble rousers identified as populists is long and intimidating: Huey Long, Father Coughlin, Joseph McCarthy, George Wallace, Ross Perot, Bernie Sanders, and Donald Trump. That these politicians cut across the political spectrum shows that populism has little to do with the left and the right politically, or with Democrats and Republicans. It also shows that a unified, radical populist vision for America, as embodied in the Omaha Platform, has entirely disappeared from American politics. Its place has been filled by an ugly caricature, still dominant today, and well summed up by populist historian Norman Pollock. The opponents of populism, Pollock writes, reasoned as follows:

> Populism did not adjust to industrialism; hence, the movement occupied an untenable historical position. . . . [B]ecause it looked backward, its long-range solutions were, by definition, unrealistic. This meant that by not comprehending the basis for its discontent, Populism was forced to search for simplistic solutions, and, ultimately, scapegoats. The result is a cumulatively deteriorating position; as protest becomes more emotional, it bears less resemblance to reality. The final image is that of a movement of opportunists, crackpots, and anti-Semites, whose conception of the world conforms to the dictates of a conspiracy theory of history. The overall consequence of this image is that Populism has been denied its traditional place as a democratic social force. Rather its significance for American history is altered so greatly that it has come to stand as the source for later proto-fascist groups, McCarthyism, anti-Semitism, xenophobia, and anti-intellectualism. . . . [T]he very term 'populistic' has passed into the working vocabulary of many intellectuals as an epithet, signifying the traits just enumerated.[18]

***

Among the casualties of this defeat was Kellogg's insight into public non-usurious credit-debt money creation. The idea of sovereign decentralized democratic debt-money issued by public banks at cost vanished from the public mind, as well as from the minds of subsequent monetary reformers. For most remaining critics of the private banking monopoly, the vacuum was filled by the idea of sovereign fiat money issued by the Treasury or a central sovereign bank. After 1896 monetary reformers remembered Campbell and the Greenbacks, not Kellogg and Macune. They seemed to have had little choice. The reformers who survived the populist catastrophe had to make their peace with the victors. The private bank monopoly over money creation had won the war and was now in command.

The victors—the bankers—were willing to allow continued public debate over all the planks in the Omaha Platform except one: the sub-treasury plan. The excision of the sub-treasury plan from public debate is perhaps the best testimony to its significance. The losers—which more generously might be called pragmatists, and who soon called themselves progressives—sacrificed radical monetary reform in order to preserve a seat at the table to advocate for their other goals. They became the left wing of the Democratic party, embraced as well by some Republicans, like Teddy Roosevelt. The surviving planks of the Omaha Platform read like the progressive wish list which took shape in the twentieth century: graduated income tax, secret ballot, direct election of senators, an eight-hour work day, nationalized natural monopolies like railroads and the telegraph, limited immigration, initiative and referendum, postal savings banks, and term limits. Progressives would add women's' suffrage, and later, equal rights, and an end to segregation.

But the bankers who retained their monopoly over money creation cared little about these issues. The relentless mechanism of usurious interest rates—skimming off wealth from the many and putting it into the hands of the few—is what mattered to them. The banking system, after the panic of 1907, came to be organized as a cartel, run by and through the largest private commercial banks, led by J. P. Morgan and the Rockefellers. The cartel gained government approval and backing with the passage of the Federal Reserve Act in 1913. The Fed has since functioned, as we've seen, as the system's central bank: a bankers' bank, a clearing house for its members, the commercial banks, who hold accounts there; it is also a source of credit for them as needed. The Fed provides an invaluable buffer between the banks and the public, absorbing the blame for unpopular policies while deflecting attention away from the interest rate practices of the banks.

New Deal legislation creating the Federal Deposit Insurance Corporation provided a further backstop to underwrite bank solvency. The Glass-Steagall Act of 1933 separating commercial banking from investment banking was presented as a regulatory constraint on banking functions, which it was; but, like so much New Deal federal regulation aimed at restricting corporate power, it ended up a blessing in disguise for the banks, curbing the dangerous speculation of rogue banks in favor of stability and steady profits. By the election of Ronald Reagan as president in 1980, rolling back federal regulation of corporate activities had emerged as a goal for both major parties. Banking regulations were loosened, most notably with the repeal of the Glass-Steagall Act in 1999. Not surprisingly, financial instability increased, first with the dot.com crisis, then the housing boom of the 2000s, followed by the collapse of Lehman Brothers and the financial meltdown of 2008, with continued asset inflation, bank instability, exploding debt levels, and stagflation.

In the wake of the 2008 crash, monetary issues reentered public debate, from which they had been largely absent since 1896. Financial analyses of banks and the crash and income inequality became best sellers, and monetary issues once more reentered mainstream debate. A revived libertarian streak associated with Ayn Rand, Alan Greenspan, Ron Paul, and others dominated conservative reactions to the new financial instability. This neoliberal reaction favored a return to something like the gold standard. The goldbugs shared with newly invented crypto-currencies a nostalgia for a relatively fixed commodity money. Bitcoin—inherently limited to a finite number of actual electronic 'coins'—came to be regarded as a kind of electronic gold, with a similar psychological appeal. Its other defining feature—the idea of direct financial exchanges with anyone, anywhere, eliminating the banks as intermediaries—had radical appeal. All monetary exchanges in the bitcoin world were reenvisioned as direct, two-party, cash transactions, with no middlemen involved. The relative inflexibility of commodity monies, however, even virtual commodities like bitcoin and other cryptos, has continued to limit their usefulness. Without the creation of new money to enable new production—very difficult with gold, and supposedly prohibited by Bitcoin—the economy would remain starved for money, as it was before the goldsmiths' discovered how money could be much more generously created.

The strongest reaction to the twenty-first-century monetary crisis came not from the gold bugs but from monetary reform movements, as we shall see in the next chapter, developed in progressive circles calling for some form of sovereign fiat money. The idea that countries issuing their own fiat currencies cannot go bankrupt and need not be constrained by borrowing and taxing—an idea made explicit by Modern Monetary Theory (MMT)—was widely and implicitly accepted by most fiat currency advocates. Like the Greenbackers before them, they aimed to overturn the bankers' monopoly over money creation and replace it with a centralized government monopoly. The populist monetary alternative of Kellogg and Macune continued to be locked out of public debate. The possibility of its revival depends on its viability as an alternative in our own time. To that end, in the last chapter, we shall outline in some detail how a populist public banking system might actually look like today. But first we will examine more closely modern fiat money theory.

NOTES

1. Frederick Jackson Turner, *The Significance of the Frontier in American History* (Martino Fine Books: 2014 [1894]), et passim.

2. For further background, see the author's previous works: *Fixing the System: A History of Populism, Ancient and Modern* (New York: Continuum, 2008) and *The*

Ecology of Money: Debt, Growth, and Sustainability (Lanham, MD: Lexington Books, 2013).

3. James K. Galbraith, "In Defense of Low Interest Rates," Annandale-on-Hudson: Levy Economics Institute of Bard College, Policy Note (July 2023): 1, https://www.levyinstitute.org/pubs/pn_23-3.pdf.

4. Ibid., 2.

5. See William Leggett, *Democratick Editorials: Essays in Jacksonian Political Economy*. Lawrence H. White, ed. (Indianapolis: Liberty Press, 1984), et passim.

6. Kellogg, op. cit., 206; op. cit., 7.

7. For a summary of the economic background of this pivotal time in American history, see David O. Whitten, "The Depression of 1893," EH.net (Economic History Association) online at https://eh.net/encyclopedia/the-depression-of-1893/.

8. Edward Kellogg, *A Treatise on the Currency and the Exchanges: Proposing a Remedy for the Evils That Exist in Relation to Them, by the Establishment of a General Exchange Office, Which Shall Also Be the Fiscal Agent of Government* (New York: Hopkins and Jennings, 1841), 5–6.

9. Ibid., 4.

10. Ibid., 6.

11. Campbell, Alexander, *The True American System of Finance: The Rights of Labor and Capital, and the Common Sense Way of Doing Justice to the Soldiers and Their Families: No Banks, Greenbacks the Exclusive Currency* (Chicago: Evening Journal Book and Job Print, 1864 [Cornell University Library Digital Collections, 2014]), https://digital.library.cornell.edu/catalog/may906923; on Campbell's divergence from Kellogg, including his rejection of Kellogg's public banking and his introduction of the interconvertible bond, see Irwin Ungar, *The Greenback Era: A Social and Political History of American Finance, 1865–1879* (Princeton: Princeton University Press, 1964), 94–100.

12. Unfortunately, these Greenbacker appropriations of Kellogg have continued to be repeated, notably in the essay "Edward Kellogg: Father of Greenbackism," by Joseph Dorfman, printed as an introduction to the 1971 republication of Kellogg's *Labor and Other Capital* (New York: Augustus M. Kelley, 1971), 5–14.

13. Lawrence Goodwyn, *The Populist Moment: A Short History of the Agrarian Revolt in America* (New York: Oxford University Press, 1978), 109–10.

14. John D. Hicks, *The Populist Revolt: A History of the Farmers' Alliance and the People's Party* (University of Nebraska, 1961 [1931]), 189–90.

15. *The Omaha Platform*. Reprinted in George Brown Tindall,

ed., *A Populist Reader, Selections from the Works of American Populist Leaders* (New York: Harper & Row, 1966), 90; op. cit., 96.

16. The full text of the 1890 bill is included in A. A. Dunning, chapter 21, "The Subtreasury Plan" in *The Farmers Alliance History and Agricultural Digest* (Washington: The Alliance Publishing Company, 1891), 336–38.

17. John D. Hicks, *The Populist Revolt: A History of the Farmers' Alliance and the People's Party* (University of Nebraska, 1961 [1931]), 194.

18. Norman Pollock, *The Populist Response to Industrial America: Midwestern Populist Thought* (New York: Norton Library, 1966), 6.

Chapter 4

Fiat Money

Since their 1896 defeat, the populists' vision of money creation through public banking has been overshadowed in both popular and scholarly debate by two other proposals for sovereign money reform that have competed as alternatives to the current private banking system. One of them—advocated by libertarians and gold bugs—would have the state revert to commodity money. It would put the monetary system back on a specie standard, preferably gold, and tie the issue of notes closely to the value of the metal in question. This reform, however, does not interfere with the operation of the private banking system; it only forces it back on the gold standard. There is no relief for borrowers, who remain entrained in the bankers private lending system. Although the gold standard functioned on and off for centuries, it proved inflexible in the face of emergencies (the Napoleonic wars, the World Wars, the Depression), when it was usually suspended, and eventually it was abandoned. Even in quieter times, a gold standard puts an arbitrary check on credit by insisting on a backing which would have its own value, but which is too rare and inelastic to provide an accurate and efficient measure for pricing goods and services. The prospects of a gold standard revival may seem remote in in a modern economy, but the persistence of its advocates, the history of gold in monetary affairs, and the enduring appeal of gold to many as a plausible explanation of the nature of money, suggests that it will remain an option in the minds of many, particularly in a time of crisis.[1] A complex society, however, needs more credit than specie can support.

The other alternative proposal for sovereign money—the subject of this chapter—calls for an unbacked government fiat currency issued to fund government expenses, and to be accepted in payment of taxes. The appearance of government fiat money historically followed soon upon the rise of the private bankers' version of credit-debt money, and was largely a reaction to it. Fiat currencies in America go back to colonial times, but the most extensive fiat money experiment in modern America was the issuance of Greenbacks during the Civil War. Fiat money today has captured the enthusiasm of many monetary reformers, particularly on the left, and especially among progressives and socialists. Fiat monetary theorists promise a second financial revolution. Just as bank money effectively replaced commodity money, they reason, so the government can now replace bank money with its own fiat money. Progressive reformers in Western countries, with confidence if not with hubris, have increasingly put their faith in unbacked fiat money. They would replace the private bankers' creation of money by the direct issuance of currency by the government to pay its bills and fund its benefits. Once the goldsmiths and others realized that money could be created *ex nihilo*, rather than first having to be discovered physically, as with commodity monies, it was but a short step to ask what necessary limits, if any, stood in the way of the simple creation of money by government command, literally by fiat alone?

Once the bankers showed how new money could be created, why, astute observers no doubt wondered, should not the state be able to do the same? Shouldn't money creation be a power of the people, not the bankers? Why should bankers enjoy a private monopoly over an indispensable and universal public function? Why should the government not provide the money we need, or it needs? Why not simply have it issued directly by fiat, or command of the state. These and similar questions were raised by some who recognized, and were shocked, by the bankers' audacious exercise of money creation. The perceived injustice of making a private profit from a public necessity resonated deeply and widely among those who understood what had happened in financial history. By and large, however, private bankers fought back subtly and tenaciously, and for the most part successfully, to retain and even extend their newfound powers, and to obscure from the general public, including the educated classes, what they were doing.

There were, however, important exceptions to their dominance. The most successful real-life alternative to modern private banking in Western countries came in Germany, where, in the nineteenth century, a widespread system of local public banks—the *Sparkassen*—was established independent of the private larger banks. The similarities with Kellogg's proposed system are remarkable.[2] The *Sparkassen* grew out of early German savings banks, beginning in Hamburg in 1778. In 1801 the first municipal *Sparkassen* was established in Gottingen, and the idea was subsequently institutionalized under state law by the Kingdom of Prussia in 1838. By the early twentieth century, thousands of *Sparkassen* were established throughout Germany, and they continue to this day as the largest sector of German banking.[3]

Unlike the smaller and more limited American savings banks, *Sparkassen* is an extensive integrated but localized network of full service, decentralized public banks, supporting both individual and commercial accounts and loans. As one analyst, C. V. J. Simpson, writes,

> [S]een from an Anglo-American perspective, they are unique. They provide not just finance but are obligated by their constitution to support the sustainable development of the total economy within their defined geographic business area. They also have very significant social responsibilities that extend well beyond provision of banking services. These Savings Banks are not state banks but are essentially credit institutions operating under public law. Their responsible public bodies (but not owners) are the local municipalities. Savings Banks are not a consolidated group; each Savings Bank is an independent credit institution and is highly autonomous. They, however, come under an umbrella organization, the Deutscher Sparkassen—und Giroverband (DSGV) that, although it can only exercise control by consent, is able to ensure effective and efficient operation with very low risk.[4]

The impressive success and resilience of German economic development since the nineteenth century can largely be attributed to the *Sparkassen*.[5] By providing low interest credit for local enterprises under local control, they have provided capital to small businesses not available in most other Western countries dominated by centralized private banking favoring large corporations. The localized structure of this kind of decentralized public banking parallels the democratic capitalism of American exceptionalism described in the last chapter, as well as the similar economic development theories associated with Jane Jacobs. In *The Death and Life of Great American Cities,* and subsequent works, she pointed to the importance of small independent businesses as the anchors of neighborhoods and communities, and as incubators of economic innovation and development.[6] She, like the American populists before her, decried the impersonality, alienation, and tyranny of large-scale social structures—public and private, government and corporate, necessary as they may be in some form. She no doubt would have appreciated how the diverse small businesses and enterprises she champions have uniquely benefited from local public banking like the *Sparkassen*.

Unfortunately, the decentralized public banking model exemplified by the *Sparkassen*, in spite of its ongoing success, has had little influence in the West outside of Germany, though it has found important, even stunning, application in China, as we shall see.[7] After the political defeat of the populist movement, Kellogg's very similar and even more comprehensive scheme of decentralized sovereign money creation also had little subsequent influence on monetary reformers. The remedies sought by more recent critics of private banking, although also calling to restore the power of money creation to the state, have sought to do so by centralizing rather than decentralizing money creation. This centralizing sovereign money movement has looked to the state to issue money as a fiat currency to meet the needs of the people and address the challenges of social justice. The public banking systems embodied in the

Sparkassen and proposed by the populists, by contrast, rely on the money creation through lending backed by the productive assets of the borrower.

Fiat money—unbacked state-issued money—has found a home on the Left, among liberals, progressives, and socialists, for whom a powerful centralized state increasingly came to represent a natural instrument to right social wrongs. The most important precedents for American fiat money were found in paper currencies issued by some of the colonies, in the Continentals of the Revolutionary War, and the Greenbacks of the Civil War. Many on the Right, however, particularly gold bugs and defenders of 'free enterprise,' were also shocked by the injustice of the bankers' monopoly. They sought a return to sovereign commodity money (gold and precious metals) in hopes of disciplining what they regarded as the excesses of private bank money creation. But the marginalization of commodity money theorists as backward-looking cranks, along with the failure, particularly in the dominant Anglo-American world, to adopt anything like the public banking proposed by American populists (and actually in part adopted in Germany), has left the fiat money movement as the principal opposition left standing to the bankers' monopoly over money creation. Confident that the state can issue as much money as needed, and with its promoters often dazzled by the prospect, the idea of fiat money on the Left became the only plausible-seeming alternative to the private bank money system. In this chapter we will analyze fiat money more closely.

***

The idea of state-issued fiat money found its fullest theoretical expression in Georg Friedrich Knapp's 1905 work, *The State Theory of Money*.[8] Knapp takes the idea that money can be created by command out of nothing to its logical conclusion. The state simply defines and produces whatever monetary units it likes (paper notes, metal coins, crypto-currencies, whatever), declares them to be legal tender, produces them, spends them into existence, and then receives the same units back in taxes and other payments. Bank money—whether public or private—is not fiat money. While bank money is properly issued only when backed by collateral and limited by specific contractual repayment obligations, state fiat money has no inherent or specified redemption value actually connected to its issuance, and so has no inherent limit of issue. Fiat simply means 'command' in Latin, and in the broadest sense of the term any currency receiving the imprimatur of the state—including the gold coins of Roman emperors and European monarchs, as well as printed Continentals and Greenbacks—enjoys the command of the state that it be accepted as legal tender, confirmed by the state's willingness to accept its own coins back in payment of taxes. But in the narrower sense used in this work a fiat currency means one unbacked by any specific resource and reliant wholly on the power of the state to enforce its command to use it. The 'backing' of the state has no specific redemption to offer a bearer of a fiat dollar. Fiat money proponents point to the social benefits of government spending (security, infrastructure, entitlements, etc.) in defense of their monetary theory. These may be provided, but they just as well may not. The point is that they do not of themselves follow from the fact of fiat government spending and may just as well be provided through traditional government means of taxation and borrowing.

A fiat currency is neither based on a commodity of inherent value (such as gold, silver, etc.), nor is it securitized by the kind of collateral which stands behind the credit-debt money that banks lend to borrowers (e.g., in mortgage contracts). Backed by nothing except the power of the state, manifested in its ability to enforce laws and extract taxes, a fiat dollar can be redeemed only by another fiat dollar. By contrast, both commodity monies and credit-debt monies of account—the two monies we have so far discussed—are based on tangible, measurable things of intrinsic value. They have in common specific (if different) objects of redemption. A fiat currency, on the other hand, is a claim on nothing in particular. Its realization is uncertain and unsecuritized, and its value may range from zero to infinity. It has no inherent conditions of redemption. A Federal Reserve Note, not redeemable in gold since 1933, is technically (in the broad sense) a fiat currency, but insofar as deposits of account created by loans are backed by productive assets, and duly extinguished upon being repaid, the bank money created by loans remains redeemable in principal in a way that Federal Reserve Notes are not.

There are further problems with fiat money. For any money system to function smoothly—for prices to be stable—the rates of money creation and money extinction have to be constantly synchronized. Fiat currencies, having no clear condition for redemption, have no reliable way to balance their creation of money with its extinction. Dollars issued into circulation without adequate means to take them back out of circulation will only multiply the outstanding claims against resources held by society, intensifying competition for resources. Both bankers' money and commodity money do a better job than fiat money insofar as they actually tie credit with debt. Taxation can be used to extinguish money, it is true, but unlike the direct one-to-one, or dollar-to-dollar, connection between credit and debt (creation and extinction) in both commodity and bankers' money, taxation in fiat money is almost entirely disconnected from its creation. The government remains free to print as much money as it likes without having to make corresponding changes in taxation, while taxes can be levied for reasons entirely unrelated to money creation. The lack of any clear relationship between fiat money and taxes makes taxation a dubious and uncertain remedy for money extinction.

Fiat money further presupposes, even more problematically, a top-down theory of money creation by a centralized government or quasi-government authority, such as a treasury department or a nationalized central bank, acting on behalf of the government, and presumably the public. The monetary authority distributes the money it creates to its first users, that is, to such parties as the government sees fit to pay directly for services and other obligations (defense contractors, the military, social programs, public works, entitlements, etc.). The money flows into the general economy as the first users turn around and spend it to fulfill their own needs. The natural advantage given to first users of government spending automatically establishes a hierarchical distribution of economic benefits and powers. Managing such a monetary system would require complex technical research and constant adjustment by experts and bureaucrats—reminiscent of socialist command economies—to attempt to determine exactly to whom and in what way and at what time and to what degree the newly created money should be distributed and how taxes should be levied. The experts would have to figure out how to reliably extinguish the money they had created. The issuing authority, as a result, will find itself making command and control decisions shaping the entire economy.

***

The earliest example of state-created fiat money, at least in the West, occurred in Massachusetts in 1690, not long after the invention of money-creation by the goldsmiths in London. It was soon followed by unbacked paper (or fiat) money in other English colonies in America, and later by other fiat currencies: the American Continental paper currency issued during the Revolution, the *assignants* of the revolution in France, and later the Greenbacks in the United States, among others. These fiat currencies were sovereign currencies issued by governments, not banks, and were backed by the power of the government in lieu of any other specified backing or collateral. All were born of challenging circumstances (revolution and war) in which neither the traditional commodity monies nor the debt-money of the bankers were available to supply vast new sums of credit suddenly and urgently needed.

The first modern unbacked fiat currency—the paper script issued by Massachusetts—was born out of adversity, not opportunity. In 1684 Massachusetts lost its royal charter and its mint when it was made part of the new Royal Dominion of New England and put under a new governor appointed by the Stuart monarchy. Historian Dror Goldberg sums up the moment of fiat money invention as follows:

> Following the Glorious Revolution, the colonists deposed the governor in 1689, established a provisional government, fought Canada, and lobbied for charter restoration. In October 1690 Massachusetts failed to occupy Quebec and returning troops demanded pay. They received debentures which stated the colony's debt to them. The government's hope for loot, tax receipts, or loans were in vain. Payments for previous expeditions had already been postponed and the government was under real threat of mutiny, desertion, and defection. Allowing troops to pay taxes with debentures was not enough. On 24 December 1690 an order authorized a committee to pay £7000 in 'bills' to troops 'who shall desire' to be so paid. Any payment to the colony (for example, taxes) could be discharged with the bills. Bills could be redeemed for specie or goods 'as the Treasury shall be enabled.'[9]

As Goldberg makes clear, officials in Massachusetts were driven by desperate circumstances to the ingenious idea of issuing an unbacked paper script in the form of anonymous IOUs denominated in small units. Massachusetts as a colony was prohibited from declaring its money legal tender. Under the briefly existing Dominion of New England, land rights had reverted to the crown, calling property ownership into question. Land therefore could not be used as backing for a currency, while reduced trade and lack of specie effectively ruled out any viable alternative. Inability to declare legal tender only made things worse. What the colony decided to do in these extreme circumstances was to issue a script in the form of an IOU only potentially (but not actually) redeemable, which could be used to pay taxes. Payment of taxes was enough, it turned out, in the absence of any alternative, to give the new currency a viably broad circulation. Here was born the kernel of fiat money.

Massachusetts monetary innovators were not looking to invent an unbacked fiat currency, though that's what they did. They were reluctantly prodded into it as a stopgap measure they would rather have avoided. They had no choice but to pay lip service to the idea that any viable currency should be redeemable, or convertible, ultimately into a precious metal like gold, or into land, or into some convenient commodity, but they went on to defer any such conversion indefinitely. Backing was dispensed with as a necessary condition for the currency. What they did was noticed. Goldberg concludes approvingly, "The success of their innovation under unique circumstances illustrates a general principle in monetary theory: it is not necessary to back money with assets, make it convertible, or force sellers to accept it."[10] Thus fiat money was born.

The theoretical justification for unbacked fiat money, in spite of the working examples of colonial fiat currencies, American Continentals, French *Assignats*, and Greenbacks, came much later, from Knapp's *State Theory of Money*. He was inspired, he tells us, by a visit to the Tyrol in 1861, where a non-redeemable paper-only local currency was in circulation. Knapp's references are almost entirely to European monetary practices, but they apply to virtually any currency at all, whether a commodity or a note, backed or unbacked. All currencies, whatever their form, according to Knapp derive their legitimacy and viability solely from their designation as final means of payment for taxes imposed by the state. It appears that the unbacked paper currency which inspired him revealed to him the monetary role of the state. Only state authority, absent any other inherent feature, he reasoned, could explain its success. A state's monopoly over force and taxation allows it alone, of all institutions, to set a standard for final payment affecting the entire community. The need to use the state's money for payment of taxes automatically creates a demand for its currency, ensuring its general use in the economy for exchanges and payment of debts.

Knapp developed a theory of money irrespective of the physical nature of any specific currency. He called his description of money chartalism, from the Latin *charta*, for a ticket or token. An inherently valued commodity like gold could function for Knapp as a token of monetary value just as much as an inherently valueless paper note or electronic entry, provided that the state accept it in payment of taxes. Its value as a commodity is incidental to its function as a fiat currency. A central bank digital currency could serve just as well as gold. As a historical matter, since simple tokens like paper bills or electronic entries have virtually no value as commodities, but are vastly more convenient to manage, they have come to be the unbacked fiat monies of choice. The idea is that such-and-such a token (perhaps a digital one) is to be accepted as legal tender, and that the state itself, after initially spending out the tokens it has created, will accept those same tokens back in taxes, to the exclusion of other possible currencies or monies. That's exactly what Massachusetts did with paper tokens in 1690. An unbacked fiat or token currency was spent into the economy to pay for the government's expenses and obligations, and at least some of it was taken back in taxes and put out of circulation or extinguished. The remainder was left as savings (or capital) circulating in the hands of the public. And so it has been with all fiat currencies.

***

Such, in essence, has been the theory and practice of fiat money. A century after Knapp, a group of American financial professionals and academic scholars promoted a movement known as Modern Monetary Theory, or MMT. This group, associated with progressive politics in the United States,[11] has been perhaps the most influential proponent of a fiat monetary policy for the country in recent years. The works of Warren Mosler, Randall Wray, Stephanie Kelton, and others are entirely on board with Knapp's insistence that the state alone can create money by virtue of its power to define what it will accept in payment of taxes. "Fiat money," as MMT founder Mosler succinctly tells us, "is a tax credit not backed by any tangible asset."[12] In the fiat money world pictured by progressive reformers we have a central state authority issuing a token fiat currency to "provision itself," as Mosler puts it. Spending, according to MMT, precedes taxation and borrowing. The money created is deposited directly into the accounts of government contractors and beneficiaries, who are its first users. It then percolates from them down to the rest of the economy. Demand for the money, they say, echoing Knapp, is secured by the requirement that it be used in payment of taxes.

Money needs to be systematically extinguished as well as created to maintain its stability in purchasing power, but it's not clear how that could happen reliably in an unbacked fiat system. Taxes alone aren't enough to extinguish more than a fraction of the fiat money issued. L. Randall Wray, in "Modern Monetary Theory for Beginners," calls the required payment of taxes the "redemption" of the money, as if taxes alone could do the job.[13] Whatever value a fiat money may have, only a fraction of the money so issued can ever expect to be 'redeemed' or recaptured by the government through taxes. The rest remains the money supply on deposit or in circulation with the public. The government can reduce the money supply, if necessary, by raising taxes or by borrowing from the public. Government bonds can take money rapidly out of circulation and only slowly pay it back. If all of the money issued were somehow taxed or borrowed back, none of it would be left in the hands of the public, as all income would be returned to the government, in which case no one would have any savings. What we can expect from a fiat currency is a continuously increasing surplus of money issued over money extinguished—a steady and potentially rapid inflation of the money supply.

In 2021, for instance, during the COVID-19 crisis, the federal government spent $6.82 trillion and received revenues (call them taxes) of $4.05 trillion, leaving a deficit of $2.77 trillion. This deficit, as understood by MMT, would be the amount of money (or credit or deposits) left in the private economy after government spending ran its course. If there is no offsetting production of new goods and services to match the increased money supply, as there was not in 2021, significant inflation will result, as it did in 2022. The assumption behind MMT is that increased spending will stimulate enough economic growth to match and stabilize the growth of the currency—an assumption which can no longer be taken for granted in an age of overpopulation and environmental limits. Their faith in spending obscures the distinction between spending on consumption and spending on investment, on non-productive vs. productive spending, and invites inflation. While MMT theorists are candid about the danger of inflation with fiat money, they point out rather disingenuously that no sovereign government, which can create its own currency, ever needs to default. It can always pay its debts, technically speaking, even if in vastly inflated dollars. But this get-out-of-jail card is no better than the disease it only pretends to cure.

MMT's chartalist notion of fiat money as an unbacked tax credit means that money is created as it is first spent into the economy by the government for whatever reason (infrastructure, defense spending, entitlements, etc.). Congress would authorize specific expenditures and the money would be duly subtracted from the government's account at the Fed and distributed through the banking system to non-government accounts of recipients as directed. The government can partially replenish its account by collecting taxes and selling bonds, but, as MMT argues, there is really no need in fact for it to do even that. There is nothing (short of a Constitutional amendment) to prevent the government from authorizing such expenditures as it wishes, without regard to deficits. The government, MMT notoriously claims, is not a household which has to balance its budget; it can spend beyond its means, as long as the money spent is productive of enough goods and services.[14] When spending outruns the productivity it stimulates, inflation takes over; but even then a government can choose to continue spending along with inflation.

Between the initial spend and the final tax, the uses of money are determined by what the public (private corporations and individuals) does with it while it remains in its hands. Since, according to MMT, government deficits are a measure of the amount of money which remains in the hands of the public, the government's deficit (which it can largely ignore) is thereby redefined as the public's asset. Debt in MMT is placed in a positive, not a negative light. Nonetheless, a dollar remains a ticket to consume, a claim against society's resources, and in that sense it remains a debt society owes to the bearer. Only if production keeps pace with the issuance of fiat money can the debt it represents hope to be redeemed. There is nothing about MMT, however, which ensures that will be the case.

MMT reformers distinguish their fiat money from the bankers' credit-debt money on the basis that it is not issued as a loan, but as a direct payment with no obligation to the receiver, who is free to spend it as he or she sees fit. They and other progressive monetary reformers like to think of money as a public asset. But the debt obligation is not thereby eliminated. Instead it is simply externalized. Fiat money, it cannot be overemphasized, is, like any other money, inherently a debt which society owes to its bearer, should he or she exercise it, for just that amount of goods or services at market price as denominated by the amount of fiat currency at hand. As Frederick Soddy, one of the more lucid monetary analysts, puts it, "Wealth is the positive quantity to be measured and money, as a claim to wealth, is a debt, a quantity of wealth *owed to but not owned by the owner of the money*" (emphasis in original).[15] Somewhere, somehow, the real wealth claimed by the buyer in exchange for money spent must be replenished. Removing the obligation to replenish resources consumed through the creation and spending of money does not remove the obligation for someone to replenish those resources if they are to continue to be available in future.

While most MMT supporters envision vigorous government spending, curiously they do not challenge the parallel power of private banks to create new money on the basis of the government's fiat money. They envision, or presume, a kind of public/private coexistence between fiat money and bank money. They take for granted that the fiat money issued by the government will be multiplied by private banking into many times its base value. While obligatory taxes create a demand for the government's fiat money, MMT argues that a similar dynamic underwrites the creation of private bank money.[16] In the latter case, the obligation taken on by the borrower is voluntary, not involuntary, as with taxes. Nonetheless, in their view debt obligations sustain the credibility of bank money just as much as tax obligations sustain that of government money. In both cases economic growth is presumed to sustain increased money creation.

MMT does not question the practice of private money creation, nor the usurious rates charged by bankers and other creditors. It accepts the role of the Fed and other central banks to stabilize the private banking system by managing and reconciling the accounts of member banks through their master accounts at the Fed. MMT is fine with the Fed setting a target interest rate (the Funds Rate) which sets the overall price of the money it lends to banks, and thereby influences the money supply. That this rate is maintained to service the banks, not the Fed, MMT takes for granted. As Mosler puts it, "In the real world banks make loans independent of reserve positions, then during the next accounting period borrow any needed reserves. The imperatives of the accounting system . . . require the Fed to lend the banks whatever they need."[17] MMT gives the government a central role and free hand in financing itself by fiat money, making it a core financial player in the economy, while at the same time leaving the private banking system virtually untouched. This new public-private partnership looks like an attempt to perfect what is already the status quo: the merger of business and government, or the corporate state.

***

More radical but so far less influential monetary reformers—like those gathered around the *American Monetary Institute*, the *Alliance for Just Money*, the public banking movement, and *Positive Money*—would take fiat money even further. Unlike MMT, they would not tolerate the bankers. They would entirely replace the privatized usurious banking monopoly with a system of fully and exclusively sovereign unbacked fiat money, payable for taxes, and issued by the government, or some designated agent thereof, as legal tender. This movement variously calls itself monetary reform, just money, positive money, sovereign money, sovereign monetary reform, or progressive monetary reform. The least misleading label might be Centralized Monetary Theory (CMT). Unlike MMT, CMT seeks to effectively eliminate private bank-money creation.

CMT grew in part out of the historical research in Stephen Zarlenga's *Lost Science of Money*, while its most detailed theoretical exposition may be Joseph Huber's *Sovereign Money*.[18] Huber offers this brief summary of fiat money: "[M]onetary sovereignty includes: 1. Determining the currency of the realm, the common unit of account. 2. Creating and issuing the money, the regular official means of payment denominated in that currency, and 3. Taking the benefit from money creation, the seigniorage."[19] CMT, eliminating bankers, would make state fiat money creation the *only* money creation system allowed. "Monetary reform," according to the *Alliance for Just Money*, "will make the money system operate like most people think it does. With Just Money, money will be created by the government for its people. New money will no longer be created by banks as credit, that is, through loans. Banks will still lend money as they do now, but they will lend money they actually have, rather than creating it."[20]

Progressive fiat money promoters, whether CMT or MMT or otherwise, are chartalists at heart. They argue that money can be freely created by fiat, or command, of the state, as Knapp insisted, and that fiat currencies are unbacked, that is, non-redeemable in anything else besides themselves. In its most radical or complete form, CMT fiat money consists in 100% state money creation, leaving no room at all for bankers' credit-debt money, or commodity monies, or any other kind of money. Joseph Huber calls this "full chartalism."[21] Total state control over money, which this would be, raises the questions of what kind of state and what kind of money. CMT reformers have rather innocently taken popular sovereignty for granted. They presume that their reforms would be realized in the context of representative governments and the rule of law. But popular sovereignty has not consistently translated into popular accountability, and the rule of law can and has been used just as well to undermine as to promote social justice. Indeed, popular sovereignty and the rule of law in recorded history have gone hand in hand with vast inequalities of unaccountable wealth and power. State power in popular governments has proven itself an instrument equally adaptable for good or evil. State power is concentrated power, and concentrated power is resistant to accountability to anything other than another concentrated power. A genuinely democratic state, by contrast, would be maximally decentralized, with concentrations of power (including money power) minimized and as directly invested in the people as possible. This was the broader populist vision.

Direct-issue, single-source fiat money in its pure form as CMT substitutes one centralized monopoly with another—the system of central bank coordinated but privately run state chartered banks is replaced with a public system run by the government. The centralized distribution of money is undertaken as a vehicle for social justice, which it certainly could be; but, lacking adequate democratic accountability, it would more likely be a recipe for favoritism, special interests, inequality, and corruption. It would necessarily be a managed, top-down financial system, and like any top-down system it would require a bureaucracy, which means the many being governed by the few. In the end, the sociologist Robert Michels's famous 'iron law of oligarchy' is likely to prevail in any hierarchical organization, where power is inevitably concentrated at the top.[22]

Fiat monetary theorists argue that a special agency or commission or monetary authority—a suitable group of experts—could somehow calculate the rate of inflation or deflation and recommend that Congress adjust taxes and state borrowing accordingly to offset undesirable increases or decreases in prices.[23] But the uncertainty of economic calculations, the divergent views of economists, the lack of full information, the power of central government agency, political polarization, corruption, and the lack of political accountability, all undermine confidence that such a central agency could hope to control inflation, or even be objective in attempting to do so. Even with determined rational agents in charge and dedicated to the public good, the calculation of how much money should be issued, and how much taxed back, would require a top-down and virtually omniscient overview of resources, labor, capital, and their interactions. Creating and spending fiat money is relatively easy, compared to getting it back out of the economy and trying to control inflation. The demand for money (once it's understood to be a 'free' creation) would be very high, and hard to deny or parse; the competition for funding among recipients, presumably left to Congress, would inevitably favor those with the most political influence, thus possibly enabling a maldistribution of wealth as bad as any other.

To prevent bankers from engaging in the private creation of money through lending at interest, CMT reformers have promoted reviving some version of the Chicago Plan of the 1930s which would prohibit fractional reserve banking and allow private lending only on preexisting deposits.[24] The credit and money creation scheme invented by the goldsmiths would finally be rolled back, and entirely replaced by government fiat money. Direct government spending would replace credit creation, with bank credit replaced by state fiat money issued directly to meet social needs. Wealth and power would flow to the direct recipients, or first spenders, of fiat money, with all others more or less dependent upon them. Individualized debt obligations would be replaced with spending allocation in a system of command finance.

The major precedent for pure fiat money in the United State is the issuance of Greenbacks during the Civil War. These were U.S. dollars issued by the Treasury Department to pay government contractors for the expenses of the war. Over $450 million were issued in an experiment hailed as a great success by most fiat monetary reformers. The government was indeed able to fund a war while avoiding borrowing at usurious rates from private bankers to do so, though the bulk of the funding for the war in the end came from government bonds, not Greenbacks. The Greenback, moreover, traded poorly against gold (the stable international currency of the day), losing as much as 2/3rds of its value at its worst, and consistently remaining well below par.[25] Further, the new money quickly became concentrated among corporations and other military suppliers, and ended up in New York banks and Wall Street speculation. Greenbacks were a desperate attempt to stave off national bankruptcy. The medicine helped to win the war, but like many medicines, it was a poison as well.

Perhaps the ultimate exercise in total fiat money came with the Soviet Union, both in its early years and in its heyday after World War II. In their attempt at a full implementation of a command economy, the Soviets ran the central planning of the entire economy from the top down through the state planning committee, known as Gosplan. They similarly ran the central planning of the entire monetary system from the top down through the state banking committee, known as Gosbank. Gosbank issued money of account to the state enterprises of production to exchange with one another to fulfill planned quotas. This state money circulated among state enterprises only through their special accounts in the state bank. Individuals had separate accounts unrelated to industrial accounts into which were deposited direct salaries for living expenses. These deposits were largely disconnected from their productive work and based instead on perceived needs. Salary income was in cash, or paper rubles, not money of account. It could only be spent or kept in personal accounts with the state bank.[26] The two money systems did not mix.

The Soviet system took fiat money to its logical conclusion. It perfected the complete dissociation of money from the economy. The idea was that the production and distribution of goods and services could be thoroughly rationalized. In such a complete, perfected system, the expectation was ultimately that virtual omniscience (approaching 100% predictability) could be achieved regarding all possible outcomes while considering all possible variables affecting all possible production and distribution. The seemingly irrational aspects of human behavior—desire, emotion, fear, insecurity, anxiety, greed, pleasure, pain, pride, and so on—would either have to be ignored or else exhaustively analyzed and made predictable and controllable, that is, no longer irrational, in order to match what the economy could deliver with what would satisfy human consumers.

In the Soviet experiment that match was never made. The goals and quotas of the Gosplan and Gosbank experts failed dramatically to meet the expectations and eventually even the needs of the consuming public. Most conspicuously, salaries overall exceeded economic output, leaving most people with more money than they could ever spend not because salaries were too high but because there was so little to spend it on. Money thus failed in its role as a measure of economic value, leading to slow-moving economic chaos.[27] Since production and distribution are dependent upon investment, or promises of future results, they are time dependent. And one of the best measures of time dependency is debt, or the specified monetary obligation of timed future repayment. Money can be a measure of production and distribution only to the extent that it can be an accurate measure of debt, and debt is precisely what fiat money tries to ignore.

***

Fiat money theorists offer their own version of modern monetary history. Christine Desan's 2014 book *Making Money*, a dense and detailed scholarly work, is often cited by other fiat money proponents as an authority. Here is one of several similar versions she offers of her story of money creation:

> 'Money' is invented when a community, acting through a stakeholder, denominates in a homogeneous way the disparate contributions received from members, and recognizes them as a medium and mode of payment. To produce money's basic structure, participants advance the time value of resources owed to the center in return for that actor's singular ability to represent those resources in units that are accountable and transferable. The units entail the fiscal value of the taxed resources, as it is enhanced by the cash quality they gain as countable, transferable markers. On the basis of money's fiscal infrastructure and in response to people's demand for cash services, societies can expand their money supplies beyond those made for public uses; they can sell money to individuals or license others to sell money to those people. Making money is therefore a material project: it proceeds by intervening into the way people relate to resources and it distributes profits and costs as it does.[28]

Here we find MMT in academic garb. What we read is no different from Mosler's account of money creation cited above. The sovereign once again creates money by spending it into circulation, where much of it continues to circulate as the currency of the land and extinguishes (some of it) by taking it back in taxes. But whereas Mosler was pragmatic and neutral about the state creating money, Desan identifies the sovereign ambiguously (and perhaps contradictorily) both as 'the center,' and as a 'community acting through a stakeholder.' The presumption of Desan, and fiat money theorists broadly, is that the community is obliged to act not individually through its citizens, but collectively through its stakeholders. The stakeholder groups and organizations are portrayed as representing the will of the people with regard to the disposition of the labor and resources of the community. The stakeholders (more or less organized collectives) are the authorities (deciders); the people, as individuals, are not authorities, and have little or no standing. They are merely units in collectives. The sovereign is the ultimate stakeholder who somehow distills these many inputs into policy, including the creation of money and the regulation of monetary practices. As she puts it, "As suggested by the historical record, money is contrived by a *group* to measure, collect, and redistribute resources. The *community* may be a *state*, but it can also be a *collective* organized along the lines of loyalty, religion, or affinity to which people make recurring contributions of labor or goods" (my emphasis).[29]

The fiat theory of money as reflected by Desan presumes imagined outcomes not warranted by the theory itself: that we expect fiat money to be created rationally, intentionally, and democratically ('contrived by a group' or a 'community') in order to 'redistribute resources.' Fiat money in her view appears as an instrument of a broader vision of social justice. Mosler, by contrast, doesn't hesitate to imagine colonial despots imposing fiat money under authoritarian rule to mal-distribute resources to themselves and their clients.[30] The neutrality of fiat money as an instrument for good or evil seems evident enough. It is indeed an instrument to redistribute wealth, ultimately a power of the sovereign, but it is the very possession of such a power which may be called into question, as the populists certainly did.

Another fiat monetary theorist, following in Desan's steps, is Jakob Feinig. His recent *Moral Economics of Money* distinguishes between what he calls "moral economies" and "monetary silencing."[31] Feinig defines the "moral economics of money" historically as necessarily involving the activities of "large groups of money users who attempted to promote a monetary design they considered just."[32] By "monetary silencing," Feinig means "the processes that reduce money users to individuals who have no role in shaping money creation."[33] He invokes the idea of 'monetary design' by which the moral economy of money can be realized. Realizing a 'moral economics of money' requires taking intentional public action to restructure the monetary system to achieve social justice. Reflecting MMT optimism, Feinig asserts that "the idea that the quantity of money in the public coffers limits what societies can do is a myth. Since money is a malleable institution, it can mobilize existing resources and build new productive capacities."[34]

Feinig and Desan, unlike MMT, both view American monetary history as a contest between private interests (the bankers and capitalists) and those (like themselves) seeking public justice through monetary reform. They rightly include the populists, in passing, among those seeking social justice, but misrepresent them as Greenbackers, and ignore their monetary centerpiece of public banking. Populist social justice is justice for the individual, not justice in the abstract. Kellogg's public banking system features no third party interposing itself in the contracts between creditors and debtors. Fiat money theorists do precisely that. Desan makes the point clearly that a fiat currency "proceeds by intervening into the way people relate to resources and it distributes profits and costs as it does" (cited above).

This is not the kind of money radical populists imagined. They did not want their representatives telling them how their own money should be created and distributed. They resisted the sleight of hand by which the trustees of the public interest slid into becoming the *de facto* owners of the public interest. They wanted to create and spend their own money themselves. The irony was that they knew what they were talking about. As businesspeople, or capitalists, they were already individually creating money as borrowers in partnership with private banks. What they wanted were non-usurious local public banks, instead of usurious local private banks, to provide them with the credit they needed. Their idea was to correlate money creation directly to individuals through public banking, and confine it there, as an exclusive right of the people.

Fiat money is the money of the state, not the people. Even if the state is believed to speak for the people through their representatives, the voice of the state (the law) can and often does diverge from, and can even contradict, the voice of the people. The state is not the people. The populists' money of the people, unlike fiat money, would not have been created and spent on behalf of the people by the state, but instead created and spent by the people among themselves, in countless individual loans and subsequent transactions. If money is truly a function of the sovereign (and not a private power), and if the people as individuals are themselves truly and fully the sovereign, and if their own personal loans are the actual source of money, then their claim to the exclusive and first use of money as institutionalized by local public banking as a matter of natural right seems hard to deny.

It remains, of course, that the people cannot represent themselves (constitute themselves an actual democracy) beyond the scope of Jefferson's Ward Republics, or face-to-face town meetings, or assemblies open to all citizens. It would take the national representatives of the people in Congress with the president's support, or a constitutional amendment, to realize whatever monetary theory on this scale any reformers might desire. What is unique about radical populist monetary theory (built on local public banking) is that it requires the sovereign power, as represented by the state, to validate the relinquishment of its own monopoly to create money for itself. The state, like anyone else, under a public banking system would have to fund itself through taxes and borrowing as appropriate. Only on the face-to-face local level, with individual borrowers going to their individual local public banks, would the state be a party to the creation of money, along with those individuals. For populist public banking to succeed, the state has to be enlightened enough to give up some of its power.

It will be objected that populist public banking is only another way to concentrate wealth and power, this time in the hands of small and mid-sized capitalists. Wealth will continue to be unequally distributed, dividing society between rich and poor, with the poor dependent on the charity of the rich since their power would be derived from government to help them. The populist could only agree that there would indeed be richer and poorer, but maintain as well that such would be the natural result of an economic meritocracy in which productive individuals justly earn the rewards of their labor. Without the engine of usurious interest rates, however, and the speculation based upon them, wealth would no longer be able to multiply automatically, but would fluctuate naturally with the level of production in response to supply and demand. Credit money tied by loans to the level of production would be stable, non-political money, not to be confused with the political money of the fiat theorists. It would remain to the citizens and their representatives to fund such social measures as they deemed necessary, only they would have to do so through taxes and borrowing, not by simply 'printing money.' If the political will to achieve social justice can be mobilized to achieve a fiat money system, why could it not be mobilized through taxes and borrowing by elected officials?

* * *

In modern fiat money systems, real or imagined, the government, in the shape of a monetary authority, interposes itself between the money system and the public. The government creates the money as it spends it. As the first spender, the government puts itself in a position to determine who the first users of any new money will be. The power of the government to influence the economy is thereby rendered concentrated, expanded, and largely unchecked. There is little or no external restraint left on government spending and taxation. Why, it might be asked, even in a Western 'democracy,' should a group of elected representatives, even with the best of intentions, be able to intervene in the creation and distribution of money in place of letting the citizens do this for themselves, as they are perfectly capable of doing? Why would anyone think they would be able to manage the affairs of others more successfully and honestly than they could themselves? Why instead couldn't money be made available *on equal terms* to every individual? That was, of course, the aim of Kellogg's monetary theory.

It is only in the case of a pure fiat monetary system that the state not only fully establishes its monopoly power over money creation but reserves to itself (as the 'representative' of the people) the exclusive right to fully exercise it. The power of pure fiat money is not delegated to anything (e.g., gold), or anyone (e.g., private bankers), but is realized and monopolized by the government itself. The state need only declare the money it decides to spend into existence, and proceed to do so, making sure that it alone is received back in taxes. A state fiat currency requires a national level of administration because only a national monetary authority can only manage the money it creates by national taxation. A monetary administration, interposed between the people and their money, would necessarily be concentrated and bureaucratic, with management in the hands of 'experts' far removed from the public eye. Ultimate responsibility may lie with Congress, but Congress for a long time has proven itself more responsive to the donors who fund Congressional campaigns than to the voters they are elected to represent. The power to control and direct the issuance of money in a centralized fiat system would inevitably be concentrated in a few hands, who would have at their disposal, with few constraints, a new and powerful instrument to carry out any agenda they may desire. Unbacked fiat money, we should remember, can serve any regime. It can be the money of a new socialism as well as that of a new fascism.

The more radical fiat monetary reformers aim to replace private bankers' credit-debt money with public sovereign fiat money. By rejecting credit-debt money as a system of money creation, they dismiss its essential virtue: the fact of making the creation of money contingent upon a promise to repay it. Bank money, or credit-debt money, neatly matches up the creation of money with its extinction. Money borrowed must somehow be destroyed in order for it to continue to be created without constant inflation. The loan contract closes that loop, with money creation (issuance of debt) automatically correlated with its extinction (repayment), whenever a loan is created. Most important, perhaps, is the precise equivalence, to the penny, between loan contracts for money borrowed and money required to be paid back, and for an exact time agreed. It is not some estimate or projection, subject to constant revision. Fiat money creation, by contrast, abolishes the loan contract and its self-regulating mechanism; it thereby disconnects money creation from money extinction, turns quantification into guesswork, and invites the triumph of desire over prudence, of imagination over reality.

There is nothing wrong with the bankers' credit money *per se*; it is simply a mechanism for expanding the money supply while still maintaining sufficient operational backing. For the goldsmiths the operational backing remained the gold in their reserves; for banks the operational backing is no longer gold in reserves but rather a legal lien on the collateral of the borrower. For modern banking—for 'the English system' as we know it today—the loan collateral is supported by taxpayer-backed government bonds and the stability of a central bank. The problem with 'the English system' lies not in the 'system' as such, but in the usurious interest rates attached by bankers to their otherwise legitimate loans. The challenge is not to throw out the baby with the bath water, but to incorporate the ingenious and effective debt-money system of the bankers into a just and fair monetary reform.

That is what the populists aimed to do. Public banking in some form—creating money through debt without usurious rates—was the deepest goal of the nineteenth century American populist monetary reformers. They were not progressives, who have been the major advocates of government fiat money, then and now. They were populists who wanted to democratize the ingenious money creating system the bankers had invented. They appreciated the bank-money system but wanted it to work for them. They aimed to end the bankers' private monopoly over banking, not to destroy banking itself. They wanted to turn credit-debt money creation into a public monopoly. They were businessmen and businesswomen—small-scale capitalists—who understood and appreciated that money was created by loans from banks. Their aim was to replace private banking with public banking. They sought a nationally standardized and coordinated system of local lending by public banks to individuals at nominal or non-profit rates of interest. They saw credit as a right due any qualified borrower, not a privilege to be purchased only at usurious rates.

The populists recognized that the public actually engages in the creation of money on a direct, individual basis, for personal use, whenever anyone takes out a loan. This is a far cry from fiat money creation by the federal government, most notably with the Greenbacks. Loans creating credit money engage in complementary money extinction through the individual repayment of those loans. Insofar as credit-debt money is created only when an individual bank and an individual borrower contract to sign a loan agreement, there is no need for upstream money creation as in fiat systems. And insofar as it is extinguished when a loan agreement is paid out, there is no particular financial need for upstream money extinction either, such as taxes. No centralized authority, no single point of issuance, is needed or required for the money to be created or extinguished. Instead it can be created and extinguished in many places at once, at the moment when it is borrowed and at the moment the loan is cancelled out.

Money creation and extinction in public banks would be dispersed and localized, the result of millions of individual loan contracts beginning and ending across the land. It would be entirely democratized. Instead of a central bank or treasury department fiat scheme dispensing vast sums top-down, public banking money would be dispensed from the ground up, through the nearest local public bank (imagine, say, one in every county, or in every neighborhood), to individuals. It would be extinguished in those same banks between those same parties. Private banks could remain free to operate; there is no need to force them to shut them down. But every citizen would now have the option of direct, low-cost, non-usurious borrowing at their local public bank. In the final chapter we will examine Kellogg's populist monetary theory in detail, and explore its unique insight into the nature of money and credit, and its promise for the future.

NOTES

1. For an interesting recent defense of gold as natural money, see Roy Sebag, *The Natural Order of Money* (White River Junction: Chelsea Green Publisher, 2022).

2. German immigrants to the American populist strongholds in the south and west may have been aware of the *Sparkassen* and could possibly have influenced the populists. Whether or not they did, the populist monetary theory of Kellogg was conceived out of the financial debates of the Jacksonian era, as well as drawn from his direct experience as a businessman trying to understand the 1837 crash, and his own experience of the creditor-debtor relationship. His work is rather remarkable in its self-generated quality as an original treatise on first principles, with few external references (and none to the *Sparkassen*). Yet the parallels of his system to the *Spasskassen* are remarkable, as we will see in the next chapter when we later examine Kellogg's proposed system of public banking in closer detail.

3. See "Sparkassen Savings Banks in Germany," *Centre for Public Impact: A BCG Foundation*, March 27, 2017, https://www.centreforpublicimpact.org/case-study/sparkassen-savings-banks-germany.

4.C. V. J. Simpson, "The German Sparkassen: A Commentary and Case Study" (London: Simpson Associates, January 2013), 13, http://www.civitas.org.uk/content/files/SimpsonSparkassen.pdf.

5. Ibid., 13.

6. Jane Jacobs, *The Death and Life of Great American Cities* (New York: Random House, 1992) et passim.

7. See Duan Kun, Plamen Ivanov, and Richard A. Werner, "Deciphering the Chinese Economic Miracle: The Resolution of an Age-Old Economists' Debate—and Its Central Role in Rapid Economic Development," *Review of Political Economy*, April 27, 2023, https://www.tandfonline.com/doi/full/10.1080/09538259.2023.2180200.

8. Georg Friedrich Knapp, *The State Theory of Money*. Mrs. Lucas, trans. (London: Macmillan, 1924 [1905]).

9. Dror Goldberg, "The Massachusetts Paper Money of 1690" (*The Journal of Economic History* 69, no. 4 (December 2009): 1092–1106, https://www.jstor.org/stable/25654034.

10. Ibid., 1104.

11. The Levy Institute at Bard College in New York State has been a major institutional center of MMT.

12. Warren B. Mosler, "Soft Money Economics," 3, http://moslereconomics.com/wp-content/uploads/2018/04/Soft-Curency-Economics-paper.pdf.

13. L. Randall Wray, "Modern Monetary Theory for Beginners," YouTube, April 25, 2018, 37-minute mark.

14. See Stephanie Kelton, *The Deficit Myth: Modern Monetary Theory and the Birth of the People's Economy* (New York: Public Affairs, 2020), chapter 1, "Don't Think of a Household."

15. Frederick Soddy, *Wealth, Virtual Wealth and Debt* (London: George Allen and Unwin, reprint 1983), 72.

16. See L. Randall Wray, *Modern Money Theory: A Primer on Macroeconomics for Sovereign Monetary Systems*, second ed. (London: Palgrave Macmillan, 2015), 5 et passim.

17. Mosler, "Soft Money Economics," op. cit., 5–6.

18. Stephen A. Zarlenga, *The Lost Science of Money* (Valatie: American Monetary Institute, 2002), and Joseph Huber, *Sovereign Money: Beyond Reserve Banking* (Cham, Switzerland: Palgrave Macmillan, 2017); see also Christine A. Desan, *Making Money: Coin, Currency, and the Coming of Capitalism* (Oxford: Oxford University Press, 2014).

19. Joseph Huber, *Sovereign Money: Beyond Reserve Banking*, op. cit., 144; see also Jonathan Macmillan, *The End of Banking: Money, Credit, and the Digital Revolution* (Zurich: Zero/One, 2014).

20. *Alliance for Just Money,* https://www.monetaryalliance.org/the-just-money-solution/.

21. Joseph Huber, *Sovereign Money,* op. cit., 143 et passim.

22. See Robert Michels, *Political Parties: A Sociological Study of the Oligarchic Tendencies of Modern Democracy* (New York: The Free Press, 1968), et passim.

23. See, for example, *The National Employment Emergency Act of 2011*, H.R. 2990, (the NEED Act) introduced by Congressman Dennis Kucinich, where the statutory mechanics of a proposed full fiat currency are laid out; see https://www.congress.gov/bill/112th-congress/house-bill/2990.

24. See Jaromir Benes and Michael Kumhof, "The Chicago Plan Revisited" (IMF Working Paper: 2012), https://www.imf.org/external/pubs/ft/wp/2012/wp12202.pdf.

25. For a detailed picture of Greenback inflation, see Wesley C. Mitchell, "The Value of 'Greenbacks' during the Civil War," in the *Journal of Political Philosophy* 6, no. 2 (March 1898): 139–67.

26. Pekka Sutela, "Monetary System, Soviet," in *Encyclopedia.com* (February 2023), https://www.encyclopedia.com/history/encyclopedias-almanacs-transcripts-and-maps/monetary-system-soviet.

27. For a detailed analysis of the Soviet system, see Janos Kornai, *The Socialist System: The Political Economy of Communism* (Princeton: Princeton University Press, 1992), especially chapter 8 on banking.

28. Christine Desan, *Making Money: Coin, Currency, and the Coming of Capitalism* (Oxford: Oxford University Press, 2014), 24; cf. pp. 7 and 43.

29. Ibid., 6.

30. See Warren B. Mosler, *Seven Deadly Innocent Frauds of Economic Policy* (St. Croix, U.S. V.I.: Valence Co., 2010), 26–27.

31. Jakob Feinig, *Moral Economics of Money: Politics and the Monetary Constitution of Society* (Stanford: Stanford University Press, 2022).

32. Ibid., 8.

33. Ibid., 9.

34. Ibid., 12.

Chapter 5

National Public Banking

This final chapter offers an outline of what a populist National Public Banking system in the United States might look like. We will try to imagine how such a system, once established, and based on Kellogg's prototype of the Safety Fund, might actually work today. How could a 1% public credit money system serve in practice in a modern economy to guarantee individual citizens equitable access to credit, and therefore to property, in fulfillment of the individual right to resources, or capital, essential to the populist vision of America? To answer this, we will more closely examine Kellogg's prototype system of public banking. He called his public banking system the Safety Fund, as we've seen, and it consisted of what he called a single national or Principal Institution, and its many Branches. After fleshing out Kellogg's system, we will compare it with the *Sparkassen* public banks in Germany to help clarify the principles of local public banking. We will also consider the Chinese adaptation of the *Sparkassen* model. But first, some background is required.

What is at stake here is a delicate point in political economy: the intersection of politics, money, and the economy. The money component is often left out of political economy, or taken for granted as neutral and unproblematic, as if money was everywhere and always the same thing. But there are different kinds of money (minimally, bank money, fiat money, and commodity money) with different consequences following from their use. How any money system is structured fundamentally determines both politics and economics. The populists understood that the usurious rates of the private bankers guaranteed the concentration of wealth in the hands of creditors. They did not, however, question the fractional reserve bank money system as such, only its privatization as a pro-profit, monopolistic cartel. They were businesspeople who accepted the practical commercial realities of credit, debt, repayment, and interest, and took for granted the creation of money on a fractional reserve basis. They understood the need to keep credit in circulation to keep the economy running, rather than sitting as cash or as money of account in deposits, and they understood that fractional reserve banking (in the modern sense of systemic reserve capital in the system as opposed to cash-in-the-vault by individual banks) was a natural mechanism for distributing credit throughout society.

The populists, as noted in chapter 3, saw their universe of small producers increasingly threatened by concentrations of power they called monopolies. They recognized the existence of natural monopolies, or industries in which high infrastructure costs and/or economies of scale made it difficult if not impossible for multiple independent producers to compete in providing the same services or products. The populist objection was not to natural monopolies as such—which they recognized as facts of complex economic life—but to their control by private interests. Natural monopolies are often found in systems or networks tying together users or consumers which depend upon them. Competitors might gain a foothold on the margins of such monopolies, due to special circumstances, but have little hope of being able to challenge the core monopoly itself. The highway system is a stock example of a natural monopoly managed by the government, without necessarily precluding private turnpikes here or there.

Any emerging activity important enough to assume a monopoly power over enough people, the populists maintained, ought to be under public control, which for them meant direct democratic control, by elected public officials where possible. They fought to recognize banks, railroads, and communications networks (the telegraph in their day) as natural monopolies appropriate for government control if not ownership. Many natural monopolies, including the most important ones like banking, involve one or a handful of enterprises, a cartel or oligopoly, characteristically controlling a relatively unique service or product not otherwise made available to many consumers. They commonly involve a single medium, somehow accessed by numerous users, like a postal system, a railroad, a highway, a utility grid, or the internet. Private ownership of the provision of the service or product of a monopoly gives the owners a chokehold, allowing them to demand a monopoly price. In the private banking monopoly, the monopoly price is the usurious rate of interest.

The solution the populists advocated was to make public, or nationalize, the ownership of the means for providing the service or product in question, while allowing non-monopolistic competition among its private users or consumers. The highways, for instance, would be run by the state, while allowing for their use by anyone, including competitive entrepreneurs such as taxis, trucking companies, or bus lines. In the case of banking, the product in question is money and the service is credit. Kellogg's public banking system would make money available at the non-usurious rate of 1% by providing loans to the public. The public are the independent individual actors, the users or customers, who are integrated by varying abstract legal entities, which variously mediate among the users. The individual actors form a first order concrete system of users or consumers; they are variously integrated by a second order abstract system of exchange and interaction, epitomized by government and corporate bureaucracies through collective, not individual, action.

***

The tension between first-order actors and second-order systems, which define and control first-order interactions, is reflected in the tension between monopolies and their users. This applies to politics as well as economics. In the modern politics of popular sovereignty, a tension arises between the second-order collective systems of representative governments, codified in law and realized in the apparatus of government, and the first-order voluntary free interactions of individuals in face-to-face democratic encounters in the local community. The populists were stubborn Jeffersonians, jealous of individual political liberty and home rule. In a time of slavery and racism and patriarchal life, they were hardly immune from such evils, over which they differed and agonized like others. But that did not prevent them from defining citizenship as they saw it on a first-order basis of grassroots democracy by real persons, with second-order institutions and powers (including natural monopolies) not only held to account by the first-order people but restructured to maximize the decentralization of power and wealth to their benefit.

The logical conclusion of Jeffersonian politics was drawn by Jefferson himself. In the correspondence of his later years, he argued that the American revolution he helped create remained structurally incomplete. The Constitution, he felt, failed to sufficiently integrate the will of the people into the policies of government. Wealthy elites (creditors) maintained political control in Jefferson's view by disconnecting local face-to-face democratic politics from representative state and federal governments. He envisioned an alternative bottom-up system of what he called confederal government, with local democratic assemblies he called Ward Republics, electing representatives to a regional or county level, with those county assemblies in turn sending representatives to the state legislature, and the state legislatures then to the Congress. Instead of choosing representatives in mass elections, they would be selected at each level in face-to-face assemblies by the votes of their peers.

Most populists did not think through the structural reforms necessary to complete popular sovereignty as Jefferson attempted to do, but they shared with him the principle of seeking to establish direct links of accountability as a basis for a democratic republic.[1] Jefferson's confederal system based on Ward Republics was a freely drawn thought experiment. Within the existing Constitutional framework, however, the confederal system minimally represents a potential reform of the legislative branch of government, particularly the House of Representatives, as well as state legislatures. A constitutional adaptation of the confederal system would subject it to the authority of the Bill of Rights, as well as the checks and balances provided by the separation of powers as a limit on abuses of legislative powers, particularly tyrannies of the majority.

The tension between first-order actors and the second-order rules they must follow is evident as well in Kellogg's system of public banking. The first-order concrete users are the local clients of any bank. They can make deposits of money they bring to the bank from elsewhere, and they can receive money from the bank by taking out loans on good collateral. They are free, voluntary actors using the mediation and money creation services of the bank. The second-order abstract aggregating and integrating entity is the banking system itself. The current private banking system is established by bank charters, banking laws, banking regulations, and so on. A public banking system would similarly be established in law. Such a second-order system sets the rules of exchange for first-order actors. In a just political economy, as the populists' saw it, following Jefferson, power had to flow from the bottom up, requiring that second-order institutions as a rule be directly owned by the public and be responsive to the demands of first-order actors.

Kellogg's public banking system identifies what he called the Branches, or local public banks, as the autonomous nodes of the system, and the Principal Institution, or central public bank, as the interface among the branches. The Branches are mediated by the Principal Institution, just as the public is financially mediated by the Branches. The Public Institution functions to provide inter-bank exchanges among the Branches, and to provide them with money as needed. Kellogg's Principal Institution is designed to function structurally much as the Federal Reserve is designed, that is, *to serve and not dominate* its member banks, who are in fact its true constituents and masters. The Branches, backed up by the Principal Institution—the entire system of the Safety Fund—would serve the needs and purposes of the public, on a non-profit, for-cost basis, not those of private owners.

Kellogg's best if brief outline of the organization of the Safety Fund, from *A New Monetary Theory*, is as follows:

> The Safety Fund may consist of a Principal Institution with Branches. The first may be located at Washington, or some other central town, and the latter wherever convenience may require. The Principal Institution should issue money only to the Branches, and they should be required to make weekly reports to the Principal of their loans, and also of the money returned to be funded. The Principal, at certain times, should report the money in circulation. For the management of the Principal, one director may be appointed by each State, and

> one or more by the General Government. The States may elect directors of the Branches by Congressional Districts, or otherwise.[2]

Today an updated name for Kellogg's Safety Fund might be National Public Banking. What he called the Principal Institution today might be called the Central Public Bank, and what he called the Branches of the Safety Fund might be called Local Public Banks. The Central Public Bank (like Kellogg's Principal Institution) would be located in Washington, DC, New York City, or some central place, and function as the clearinghouse and backstop for the network of Local Public Banks spread across the country (imagine at least one or more in every county).

The most fundamental responsibility of the Public Banking system would be to establish a fixed measure of money to be codified in law. The measure of money, according to Kellogg, is set by a specific rate of interest it can command, just as the measure of a foot is set by a specific measure of length it commands, a pound by a specific measure of weight it commands, and so on. A variable rate of interest is no more a coherent measure of the value of a dollar than a variable foot can be a coherent measure of length, a variable pound a coherent measure of weight, and so on. What is needed, he argued, is an invariable, not a variable, rate of interest on money, just as we need an invariable length of foot, an invariable weight of a pound, an invariable time of an hour, and so on.

To be invariable, the rate of interest must be permanently fixed, and remain unchanging. It was argued in chapter three that the natural rate of depreciation over a human lifetime is approximately 1%, and that this natural rule of thumb would be a logical choice to establish as the fixed rate of interest by law, as Kellogg proposed. Under a 1% rule, as we've seen, our reinvestment rate will fall below what is needed to ensure the replenishment of the resources we consume; and above 1%, income will be usuriously appropriated from the credit-seeking public. Any rate over 1% will take wealth out of the hands of borrowers and give it as *unearned* income to their creditors. By permanently fixing by law the rate of interest at the natural rate of depreciation over an average human lifetime, or 1%, the value or cost of money would finally be stabilized, ending the radical fluctuations in value which have plagued monetary history.

Today, given the ever greater use of money and credit as measures of value central to economic production, the Central Public Bank would presumably stand alone as a federal agency. Kellogg's prototype, the Principal Institution, was designed to be a federal agency run not by federal appointees, but by officials selected by the states. This novel organization even today would be singular among federal agencies otherwise run by federal-level appointees. State selection of its governing officials aimed to ensure that the Central Bank remained autonomous in its operations and functions, and as independent of the rest of the federal government as possible. It would also help ensure the uniformity of its authority and responsibility across the country. Regarding what today would be Local Public Banks, Kellogg wrote, "The States may elect the directors of the Branches by Congressional Districts, or otherwise."[3] Local Public Banks, in short, would be run by locally elected officials. Here is evident the populist vision of bottom-up political accountability.

The primary operational role of the Central Public Bank, following Kellogg, would be to distribute Public Banking Dollars directly to Local Public Banks as needed, upon their request. These would be held as fractional reserves by Local Public Banks to support the transactions occasioned by their outstanding loans to the public. Local public banking dollars would be either cash on hand (denominated physical coin or paper bills) or money of account, available upon demand in cash, but that demand presumably would be seldom exercised or necessary. Just as commercial banks today use the Fed as their bankers' bank, so would the Local Public Banks use the Central Public Bank as their bankers' bank. The reserves provided to Local Public Banks would establish the baseline of equity necessary to anchor their main purpose: fractional reserve lending to the public. The Central Public Bank would transmit physical cash as needed to Local Public Banks, and, via their accounts at the Central Public Bank, it would also supply them with most of their needed reserves as money of account, redeemable upon demand in cash. Public Banking Dollars, whether Federal Reserve Notes or money on account, would be good for taxes and all final payments, and as legal tender for all debts.

Unlike Federal Reserve Notes, Public Banking Dollars would be issued to the public *only* by Local Public Banks, and *only* on condition as loans to individuals at 1% interest backed by good collateral. The money created by the loan would appear as a deposit in the borrower's account. The condition of issuance as loans on good collateral to be repaid by the public gives Public Banking Dollars the backing they would otherwise lack. This is why they are *not* fiat money. Kellogg makes the point in the context of the still mainly agricultural world of his day: "To make this currency a true representative of property, the Safety Fund must issue its money only in exchange for mortgages secured by double the amount of productive landed estate."[4] This was true of the most successful colonial currencies—in Pennsylvania and Massachusetts—when they were backed by land. Insofar as they were, they were not fiat currencies. Today, the definition of collateral may be expanded to include any potentially productive asset, not just land. Public Banking Dollars would be the cash basis of public bank money, which is created and multiplied in the same way as private bankers' money, with the difference that it is lent non-usuriously into the economy.

The money supply in Kellogg's financial system would be stabilized primarily by the repayment of loans, insofar as the money extinguished by repayment approximately matches the money originally created by those loans. He also envisioned that Safety Fund Notes, his version of government bonds, issued at a slightly discounted rate, would provide a means for holders of Public Banking Dollars to store their money, while at the same time funding Local Public Banks. The Central Public Bank would be the vehicle of collective self-regulation by the Local Public Banks to enforce the uniform application of their own standards among themselves, relying as necessary on reports, inspections, and the like. The welfare of the Local Public Banks would be the major concern of the Central Public Bank. The Central Public Bank would enforce such reserves or other requirements as desired by the Local Public Banks to manage their lending and mutual exchanges; it would set the proportion of reserves required to stabilize their fractional reserving banking. It would offer loans to Local Public Banks as needed. It might also require Local Public Banks to contribute to an insurance fund to cover deficits as needed. It would not, however, otherwise directly spend or borrow money. In this way it differs fundamentally from modern central banks.

Local Public Banks would reconcile their transactions among themselves through their accounts at the Central Public Bank. The Central Public Bank would act as a routine clearing house for exchanges among Local Public Banks, much as the Federal Reserve does now, including the clearing of accounts, as well as the coordination of common operating procedures, including the coin and physical notes made available to the Local Public Banks. Local Public Banks would be run in compliance with uniform standards of eligibility, collateral, and so forth, set for all borrowers by the Central Public Bank, presumably upon the advice and guidance of Local Public Banks. Anyone should be able to walk into any Local Public Bank anywhere in the country and access the same financial services on the same terms, including withdrawals of cash in dollars in the form of Public Banking Notes.

Credit-money gains its flexibility and power from the principle behind fractional reserve banking. The creation of credit money of account backed by the repayment and interest obligations of borrowers is limited only by the willingness and ability of borrowers to borrow. At the same time, any bank must hold reserves in some form to honor withdrawals of depositors, whether in cash or as transfers to accounts held in other banks. Originally this was gold in the goldsmith's vault, and today it is such capital as banks are able to hold as equity against such withdrawals. Fractional reserve banking in this broad sense provides a useful method by which to calculate the risks of lending against some amount of required reserves. The percentage held back as reserves to cover losses on bad loans will vary from time to time and place to place, but commonly accepted and enforceable reserve limits are essential to any stable banking system.

Modern credit-debt money banking is what makes it possible to borrow against the future, instead of only the present. Operationally, in terms of basic services (checking accounts, deposits, etc.), public banks would *not* differ from private banks. Private banking could even remain untouched if public banking were introduced, but it would lose its lending and money creation monopoly, which it would have to share with public banks. The challenge to private banking would be to compete with public banks offering the same services to the public at the natural rate of interest of 1%. In that competition, the natural monopoly of public banking would in effect render private banking superfluous. It would destroy its business model. At 1% the borrower gets to keep the difference between what he or she would have to earn to pay off the loan at 1% versus what it would take at any higher rate. The value of that difference—and this is crucial—accrues to the borrower, not the lender. Although the principal on loans is extinguished as it is repaid, the 1% interest would be retained by the Public Bank. It represents the fruits of production the borrower owes back to the community to ensure its sustainability.

***

Imagine a Local Public Bank in your neighborhood. It would have an office, tellers, loan officers, check books, phone apps, and an ATM, like any other bank you've seen. It would offer loans at 1% to the public for any purpose (business, education, home ownership, transportation, even luxuries), provided adequate collateral is provided. Loans would themselves be collateralized, but the 1% cap on interest would eliminate traditional speculation and keep loans closely tied to the productive assets backing them up. The standards for borrowing would be uniform nationally, enforced by the Central Public Bank, but set upon consent of Local Public Banks, and available as a right of citizenship to be exercised at any Local Public Bank. Loan collateral might be defined as broadly as may be prudent, including the potential for future earnings or other income. Since money is created through lending, the natural and only limit on loans is the number of willing borrowers with adequate collateral. In other words, the assets of a community—its land, buildings, businesses, and the labor potential of its citizens—provide the limits of what can be capitalized for the benefit of borrowers.

Public Banking would be decentralized. Money would percolate up from thousands of Local Public Banks, rather than flowing downwards from a single national source. With Public Banks dispersed across the country, and exercising locally what would be a nation-wide monopoly of money creation, money would be equally available on a transparent basis in any community to any qualified borrower. The top-down model of fiat money creation, on the other hand, privileges the first users of the new money, not the public in general; first users means a relatively small group of government contractors above all (as in defense spending, for instance), and such recipients of social welfare and other disbursements as the government may choose to make. Public Banking by contrast divides up the power of the first use of new money and distributes it into the hands of the people, that is, the individuals who actually constitute the general public, who become the first users of money, and whose communities become its automatic beneficiaries.

Public Banking would be self-regulating in the sense that money creation (loan credit) and money extinction (loan repayment) would fluctuate consistently with economic conditions in the region of any particular Local Public Bank. Local Public Bank A might have among its borrowers some whose investments of borrowed money have added to the productivity of the local economy and the prosperity of the community. For instance, someone among Local Public Bank A's borrowers might invent the widget to end all widgets, with expanding production of the new widgets creating jobs and underwriting the growing prosperity of the community. Local Public Bank B, in a separate region, might not be so lucky; it might have fewer and smaller loans, and no economic breakthroughs, and perhaps more defaults. As a result there will naturally be more money in circulation (more claims on wealth) in the community served by Local Public Bank A, and less in the community served by Local Public Bank B. There will be comparatively richer and poorer communities. *But this difference will be based on natural economic conditions, not on the usurious extraction of wealth by creditors.*

There will be other differences among local branches as well. Local Public Bank C may serve a rural community with few borrowers; Local Public Bank D may serve an urban center with many borrowers. Local Public Bank C, with a clerk or two and a small office, may look like a rural post office, with a few mailboxes and a part-time postmaster. Local Public Bank D, on the other hand, in a large building with rows of offices, and long lines, and numerous loan officers, tellers, analysts, and other officials, may be like a large central urban post office serving a large volume of clients. The former may have $100,000 on deposit; the latter may have $100,000,000 on deposit. But, as with the post offices, the various Local Public Banks would provide exactly the same basic services irrespective of their size.

The self-regulation of money means that it is created and extinguished so as to automatically match the ups and downs of economic activity. Self-regulation is inherent in the nature of any money issued as debt to be repaid insofar as each dollar borrowed is contractually pledged to be repaid on condition of forfeiture of collateral. The 1% interest covers the natural rate of depreciation, as already argued, leaving the economy in a steady state of natural activity, with natural ups and downs. Any borrower, it should be recalled, makes the assumption that he or she (or some subsequent third-party owner of the debt) will be productive enough (enriching the economy through the earnings of their labor or capital) to repay that debt (or its equivalent). The obligation to repay the principal is an obligation (on someone's part) to earn enough from the proceeds of his or her production to satisfy the debt. There is necessarily a dimension of uncertainty involved, with experience putting to the test the resolve of the borrower to pay the debt.

To reiterate, National Public Banking incorporates as its basis for money creation the local issuance of individual loans, a central feature of modern financial life which has been already established by the private banking system, but which now would be shorn of its major abuses, above all usurious interest rates. Money would not be created top-down by a centralized issuance of some sort by the government, as advocated by most fiat-money reformers, but bottom-up by thousands of decentralized borrowers in thousands of separate, discrete contractual loan transactions. Money would similarly be variously extinguished as loans are repaid. The process would be self-regulating insofar as no central authority would be required to manage and match-up money creation with money destruction.

The exclusive creation and extinction of money through local lending by Public Banks, as envisioned by Kellogg, should be as uncontroversial as the rules of traffic, or standard weights and measures, or counting votes, or buying tickets to a ball game. Money would be made available only locally, only to individuals, and solely on condition of collateral and risk assessment, with a naturally compensating rate of interest for the resources consumed in spending the borrowed money. The value or quality of money would be fixed by 1% interest on all loans, but the quantity would fluctuate with the level of economic activity. These factors together should guarantee a stable currency.

One of the strongest points in favor of a system of Public Banking as herein described, and as originally envisioned by Kellogg and his followers, is its exclusive availability only to individuals, or partnerships of individuals (or natural persons), and not to corporate groups or organizations or any other indirect and more or less abstract entities (or juridical persons). Accounts at Local Public Banks would be open only to individuals, or groups of individuals (or partners). The democratic way of distributing money is to give it in the first place to natural persons, or qualifying citizens, on an equal basis, among whom it will then circulate to smooth the wheels of production and commerce. States based on popular sovereignty are, after all, composed exclusively of real individuals, not artificial ones. The issue of corporate personhood is beyond the scope of this work, but populists and other critics have long objected to the introduction of artificial persons as interfering with the exercise of rights by natural persons.[5]

***

The populist system of public banking as examined in this work appears to have been largely if not wholly independently developed and promoted by Edward Kellogg and his followers in the People's Party, including Charles Macune, Leonidas Polk, Ignatius Donnelly, John A. Pickler, and Thomas E. Watson. We noted earlier that a similar system of public banking was established in Germany at the same time, through government sanctioned networks of local savings banks, or *Sparkassen*. There is in fact a wide spectrum found in many countries between the extremes of pure public banking and pure private banking, including cooperatives, building societies, mutuals, credit unions, postal banks, community banks, savings and loans, stakeholder banks, and others.[6] When public banking does appear in otherwise private banking dominated countries, the price for tolerating it appears to be an unofficial understanding to limit the public banking market to the smaller 'stakeholders,' meaning retail banking up to and including small businesses, while leaving large-scale corporate financing to the bigger private banks. The private bankers have permitted a degree of public banking with the hope, no doubt, of containing it. They have so far succeeded, but what they have allowed, particularly in Germany, also reveals the potential power and virtue of public banking.

What does public banking mean today? A good example of the modern aspirational vision for public banking can be found in a recent report for the British Labour Party, *A New Public Banking Ecosystem*, by Christine Berry and Laurie Macfarlane. They write,

> [W]e need structural change to reorient the banking system towards serving the public interest. This means promoting new banking models at different scales—national, regional and local—which are mandated to serve the public interest rather than simply to maximise returns. These banks are often referred to as 'stakeholder banks'—an umbrella term referring to any bank which is run in the interests of a wider group of stakeholders rather than only in the interests of shareholders. This includes public banks, co-operative banks, mutuals and building societies, as well as credit unions and responsible finance providers. There is now strong international evidence that stakeholder banks perform better than shareholder banks on a wide range of measures: they lend proportionately more to the real economy, (including small business lending), maintain larger branch networks, produce more consistent and less volatile returns, have safer business models with higher loan quality, and are less likely to fail or cut back lending in times of crisis. There is also evidence that the presence of a robust stakeholder banking sector improves wider economic outcomes such as reducing regional inequality and enhancing resilience to economic shocks.[7]

Berry and Macfarlane propose in their report a two-tiered public banking system. The first tier is to be a grassroots system of what they call local Post Banks, "to provide a full range of retail banking services" to be run through British post offices. These banks would be separate legal entities "owned under a public trust model whereby ownership is held in trust for the public benefit." They would be "governed by a Board of Trustees, comprising elected public representatives, and relevant national and regional stakeholders." Perhaps most importantly, the "Post Bank would be set up in a decentralized structure, with lending and decision-making devolved to a series of regional offices."[8] The second tier of their public banking proposal is what they call a National Investment Bank "given a broad mandate to support the government's industrial strategy, through the use of repayable financial instruments." A key role of the National Investment Bank would be to "on-lend via bank intermediaries for customers that are small businesses. On-lending should be used as a tool for promoting wider structural change . . . by lending through favoured institutions, such as Post Bank. For medium and large firms, infrastructure projects and venture capital investments, the NIB should lend directly."[9]

In their analysis of decentralized local banking models, Berry and Macfarlane make a key point—which the populists would have appreciated—about the importance of face-to-face encounters in what might be called the living democracy of everyday life, including banking, and not just the voting booth:

> Centralised, hierarchical banks have greater incentives to rely on 'hard' information which is easier to store and communicate within the organisation, while more decentralised banks are more able to make use of 'soft' information of the kind which underpins relationship lending. The more layers of hierarchy a local loan officer must go through in order to gain approval for a lending decision, and the further these decision centres are from the local branch, the less able the bank is to make use of this information—and the less likely they are to build supportive lending relationships with SMEs [small and medium sized enterprises]. Evidence also suggests that trust is a key component of the resilient lending relationships developed by banks such as the German Sparkassen, which again implies a high degree of importance for face-to-face relationships with local loan officers who are empowered to make lending decisions.[10]

The largest public banking system in the West, the German *Sparkassen*, is widely credited as an essential factor in shaping and sustaining the astonishing growth and resilience of the modern Germany economy. With assets of over a trillion Euros and hundreds of local banks with thousands of branches employing hundreds of thousands of people scattered all across Germany, the *Sparkassen* have helped make possible the unique infrastructure strength of the German economy. The precedent of public banking represented by the *Sparkassen* has not found widespread imitation in the West, but it has been reproduced with spectacular results in China. As argued by Richard Werner and his colleagues, Kun Duan and Plamen Ivanov,[11] it was the decision of Deng Xiaoping and the Communist Party leadership in 1978 to integrate the *Sparkassen* model into the Chinese state banking system which made possible the unprecedented explosion of economic growth by which China in a generation passed from a largely poor, peasant-based agricultural economy to the largest industrial economy in the world, with a rich and prosperous middle class.

As they tell the story, Werner and his coauthors explain public banking on the German-Chinese model in terms of the old debate between the Currency and Banking school originating in nineteenth century England (see chapter 1). The Currency school's main point of contention, they observe, "is that credit creation is a public privilege: the excessive privatized profits from money printing must be returned to national coffers," while the Banking School has insisted that "elastic money supply by a decentralized [private] banking system is key for robust economic growth."[12] What the Germans, and the Chinese on a larger scale, have done is to make credit creation public once more, as the Currency school envisioned, but rather than centralize it as an exercise in fiat national monetary distribution (something like Greenbacks), they have decentralized it as elastic and dispersed credit creation of bank money by a public banking system.

The Chinese began with the centralized model of state credit creation they inherited from their Soviet predecessors, with the Peoples' Bank of China initially operating like the Gosplan did in the Soviet Union. When Deng Xiaoping sought to explore ways of recovering from the economic catastrophes of the Maoist era, he resisted both the idea of public centralization of credit (still the holy grail of leftist reformers in the West) as well as the corporate banking, free market, private enterprise options promoted by the West. Instead, the Chinese government, as Werner and his colleagues put it,

> [T]o supply the nation, in particular, the liberated private entrepreneurs and enlivened SOEs [state owned enterprises], with bank credit, the central government oversaw the establishment of thousands of city and rural banks to reinforce the domestic regional competitiveness. The list includes more than 100 regional ('city commercial') banks and over one thousand rural commercial banks, each forming a pillar in the Chinese banking system. Public money creators servicing the growing financial needs of an increasingly sophisticated industrial complex mushroomed.[13]

The principal reason for the success of decentralized public banking is linked to what Werner elsewhere calls "disaggregation," the separation of credit for financial speculation from credit for productive enterprises.[14] The traditional, quantitative theory of money looked at deposits rather than credit, according to Werner, and was therefore unable to reliably correlate money amounts and flows with actual economic activity. Measuring money in terms of credit flows rather than totals of deposits and cash, proved far more revealing of the role of money in the economy. Decentralized public banking in places like Germany and China is intentionally and directly aimed at providing credit for productive resources, not speculative investments. Unlike most Western countries, where productive and speculative lending have remained obscured and confused, to the detriment of the former and advantage of the latter, decentralized public banking aimed at local productive investment in Germany and China have minimized speculation and vastly redistributed assets among the general population instead of concentrating it in a few hands. Similarly, Kellogg's 1% fixed interest rate, by eliminating usurious rates, removes the major mechanism of speculation, leaving productive assets as the main source of collateral for loans.

In most Western economies, especially in Anglo-American countries, private banking remains dominant, even on the local level, albeit with some competition from non-profit semi-public banks, such as co-ops, credit unions, and savings and loans associations. Public banking is virtually non-existent in Britain and the United States. The sole state public bank in the United States is the Bank of North Dakota. By contrast, in Germany and now in China, vast public banking systems fund robust networks of small and medium-sized businesses—the *Mittelstand* in Germany—responsible for much of the innovation and expertise of economic production.[15] Germany's political economy, in contrast to the free market economics of Britain and the United States, has long been one with a strong dose of strong state socialism (the Prussian origins of the *Sparkassen* predate even Bismarck's famous social welfare programs), currently continued in its 'social market economy.' China has had an ever stronger tradition of state socialism: actual communism. In Germany, after the failure of the post–World War I communist revolution, capitalism and socialism arrived at a kind of accommodation, whose feature has been a rebalancing of private capitalism with the public interest. The Chinese economic miracle grew out of a similar rebalancing, but coming from the other direction, with a partial reduction of central planning authority.

In both Germany and China, we find realized the same two-tiered system of public banking envisioned for Britain by Berry and Macfarlane—what they call the Post Bank for retail public banking, including small- and medium-sized businesses, and the National Investment Bank for big corporate clients. In Germany the *Sparkassen* do the retail/small business public banking, and the Deutsche Bank and other banks do the big corporate clients. The large private banks retain for themselves the centralized order of corporate finance, while the public banks finance the decentralized order of small and medium businesses. In China, public banking is a similar small-scale/large-scale hybrid. Werner sums it up as follows:

> Over the past four decades the Chinese banking system was . . . transformed from a near-monobank system to a four-pillar system consisting of (1) state-owned commercial banks (SOCBs), (2) joint stock commercial banks (JSCBs), (3) city commercial banks (CCBs) and (4) rural commercial banks (RCBs). Nevertheless, the state remains a major shareholder in most bank enterprises. A significant interest is held in the five SOCBs through China's sovereign wealth fund. The Ministry of Finance and other SOEs also hold equity stakes in the 5 SOCBs, which hold more than half of the assets in the country. The public interest in each is in the vicinity of 60 to 90 per cent. The 3 new PBs are wholly-owned government firms. The CCBs are under public control through controlling stakes held by the central / local governments. Consequently, as a majority shareholder in the bank system, the CCP appoints the senior management in all these key capitalist institutions for economic growth. Thus the majority of China's banks can be classified as public banks.[16]

This two-tiered system of public banking is common among public banking reformers, including the Public Banking Institute in the United States. Its founder, chair, and chief spokesperson, Ellen Brown, in her book *Banking on the People*,[17] imagines public credit to be made available to the people by allowing individuals to hold deposit accounts at the Federal Reserve, where they could borrow money. She also imagines governments having their own public banks as well, like the existing public Bank of North Dakota, and presumably corporations, along with communities having local public banks, while the Fed would become the public bank for the federal government. First-tier or retail banking would be conducted through individual accounts at the Fed; second-tier institutional or wholesale banking would be conducted through the interactions of federal, state, and local banking, these now all being versions of Berry and Macfarlane's National Investment Bank, now for Brown operating on a variety of levels (geographic, social, industrial, political, labor, minority, etc.).

***

A two-tiered (or multi-tiered) public banking system is a compromise Kellogg, Macune, and the democratically committed populists would have rejected. Small enterprises in the two-tiered scheme are well funded, to be sure, but large enterprises continue to be funded as well, and independently so, and to have major influence on the government. The populists were antimonopolists who objected to any unfair distributions of wealth based on privileged credit access. They would not likely have tolerated the degree of private banking such as has remained in Germany in spite of the *Sparkassen*, or the degree of state centralization and control of banking for larger enterprises which has remained the case in China after Deng Xiaoping's reforms. For the populists, by contrast, there could only be one money system, not two (or more) separate if parallel systems. A fully democratic public banking system for populists would have to be a singular, unitary public banking system, a true natural public monopoly. It would have to be personal, not corporate, public, not private.

In Kellogg's view it would be the system of the Post Bank, or his Local Public Banks, writ large. There would be no National Investment Bank, no two-tiered system. The work of the National Investment Bank—the investment of large funds in large enterprises—would be absorbed in the work of the Local Public Banks. Inevitably, some Local Public Banks, say in lower Manhattan or in other large financial districts, would receive loan requests for large sums for large projects. But, according to populist public banking, these would have to be requests by actual human persons (running sole proprietorships or partnerships), not requests by abstract corporate entities with fictitious corporate personhood. Real life representatives of corporate 'persons' would be disallowed from seeking public credit. Populist public banking would be the death knell, not of capitalism but of corporate capitalism. It would restrict the circulation of money to real individuals and in that sense would be the epitome of classical American liberalism of individual freedom. Money as credit is money in circulation because most borrowers will be spenders. Money on deposit is money not in circulation, but on the sidelines as savings. Money in circulation drives the production and service economy. Money on deposit represents the reserves of the production and service economy which can still be commanded, or how much credit there remains if needed.

The implicit challenge to corporate personhood, and the corresponding liberation of actual persons, is perhaps the deepest point reached in populist political economy. Populists were farmers and tradesmen and mechanics. They were producers. They were engaged every day in direct physical and mental efforts in discharging the demands of their businesses. They presumed and understood the labor theory of value. They understood value not in terms of countless and irregular hours, or the clock, but, like any businessperson, in the demand for their products when they brought them to market, which reflected their usefulness. The time required to complete a task was not the measure of its value. The producer's time was already his or hers to begin with, not pledged elsewhere. Only with the rise of factory workers and the hourly wage in the industrial revolution, in a context where workers focused on specialized, repetitive tasks, did labor begin to be priced in time. Only then did the time required to complete a task become the measure of its value. The labor theory of value was emptied of its contents and rights in return for being priced in hours alone, the lowest common denominator.

These are very different measures of labor value. The populist theory of value was not that of time (e.g., 'time is money') but of use. At the opening of *Labor and Other Capital*, Kellogg writes,

> Value consists in *use*; it is that property, or those properties, which render anything useful. A house that could not be occupied would be worthless, unless its materials could be employed for some other purpose. . . . The value of all property is estimated by its *usefulness*. For instance, the income that a city lot can be made to produce, determines its value. The interest on the money that its improvements will cost, must be first deducted, together with the taxes, insurance, and repairs necessary to keep the improvement permanently good. The surplus it will yield after making the deduction, determines the true value of the lot."[18]

Populism, as is evident throughout the movement, was personal capitalism, not corporate capitalism. It was the exercise of what was understood as a right of natural law for men and women to use nature as necessary to live and flourish. For the populists, this was not a right to be delegated to corporate or government entities, or anyone else, but reserved to living individuals, or natural persons. To them, governments as well as corporations posed a threat of monopoly power. Both existed abstractly, as a matter of law, represented by private individuals who were empowered to act, not in their own names, but in the name of public or private institutions they represented. Representative institutions were a necessary evil for populists, but insofar as they were unavoidable, the populists aimed to neutralize them by structuring them to automatically redistribute powers and benefits back to individuals. Kellogg's monetary system is the perfect example of a kind of self-regulating system: the actual creation of money—so often assumed to be the affair of a national government or central bank—takes place instead in countless distinct personal loan agreements between individuals and their Local Public Banks. There is no opportunity for the government to create money for its own purposes, and no need, since these same purposes are now given back to the people, who are (or should be) the government.

***

The advantage of fractional reserve credit-debt money over its competitors since the time of the goldsmiths has been its ability to sustain a much larger stable money supply. It alone of monetary systems has been able to create and extinguish money in line with the natural fluctuations in the economy. It is only fractional reserve banking which makes credit-debt or bank money possible. Further, the relatively decentralized system of private banking (even today there are thousands of independent banks in the United States) creates money without the need to manage the supply of money through a central agency, or a committee thereof, periodically meeting and deliberating face to face. There is no need for macro-financial decision making, whether it's the Fed acting in the name of the private banks or the Treasury issuing fiat dollars. Any such single point of financial monopoly power would be dissolved by populist Public Banking into millions of countess local decisions made by individual borrowers at their local Public Banks.

There is nothing about National Public Banking which would prevent government spending for any purpose it chose. The government, however, in contrast to the visions of MMT or CMT, would have to budget like a household. It would have to raise money by taxing and borrowing, as most people think it always has. It would, over time, have to balance its budget, including payments on its loans. The social justice aspect of populist money is that it be stable in value and that it be available (as credit) on an equal basis to anyone who can meet common standards of good collateral. But society as a whole would benefit. As Kellogg put it,

> [A]little reflection will make it evident that the abundant supply of money and the reduction of the rate of interest will be of equal benefit to those who are without property . . . The owners of land will obtain loans from the Fund, either to purchase property, or to discharge debts, or to pay for labor; and all the money borrowed for these purposes will go into circulation and be used by others.[19]

Kellogg's fundamental means for ensuring the democratization of money creation was to confine its issuance to natural persons at local or community branches of the public banking system. If money falls under the authority of the sovereign, and if government is based on popular sovereignty (constitution, elections, representatives, rule of law), then, as Kellogg and most populists reasoned, money creation is a right of the people. Such rights as are delegated to the representatives of the people are only those which cannot be exercised by the people themselves. Money creation, however, is among the rights already demonstrated to be exercised by the people. There is nothing about the creation of money which requires that it be a power reserved for the government (even elected representatives) to exercise in the name of the people. The fact that money created through chartered lending institutions requires the contractual cooperation of individual borrowers should remind us that individuals not only have a right to the benefits of money creation, but that they are in fact an equal part of that process, and fully deserve its benefits. Individuals today create money through their role as borrowers, and National Public Banking would ensure that they could do so without being exploited by private banks and usurious rates.

Unlike socialist and progressive critics of the status quo, who then as now have blamed capitalism for their ills, populists saw the root problems of society as caused by monopoly powers of any sort, including the money power, and not by capitalism as such. They strove to preserve capitalism as an economic practice available to ordinary citizens, and to oppose monopolistic tendencies. They lived, of course, in a world where most production was decentralized, where most people were primary producers of one sort or another (farmers, mechanics, artisans, shopkeepers, manufacturers, etc.). That world no longer exists due largely to the triumph of the very monopolistic forces the populists so fiercely opposed. In the meantime, one-time private entrepreneurs who once dominated the economy have been turned into an army of wage-laborers, entirely dependent on the prospects for employment. Nonetheless, even though small businesses have shrunk to about 40% of the economy, they remain an overwhelming 99% of all businesses.

Curbs on monopoly power, including monopoly power over money, are necessary in the populist analysis to sustain and invigorate small scale capitalism and redistribute assets, credit above all, equitably. A monopoly in any industry or economic sector makes possible the extraction of unearned income from the public (users or consumers). Usury may be the ultimate in unearned income, but monopoly pricing in any form guarantees that profits will reflect not the prices set by competition, or the costs of materials and labor, but those set by the monopolist. Earned income is associated with labor, and unearned income with its absence. Labor is a debt for services which is settled in payment as wages, salaries, self-employed income, or other payments for labor, such as tips. Income from interest and capital gains by contrast is unearned income.

The mark of a monopoly (which can be an oligopoly, or a cartel or consortium of monopolists) is its ability to extract unearned income by controlling a market. The populists had little hesitation about using state power to own and manage monopolies. They repeatedly called for the nationalization not only of banks, but of the railroads and telegraph systems, much as the highways and canals and postal services even in their day were already nationalized to varying degrees. These so-called natural monopolies were to be operated as public conveniences to facilitate (not obstruct) competition among non-monopolistic capitalistic producers. The fruits of natural monopolies were to go to the people. They were not intended as centers of independent power but as government agencies or bureaus serving the public, run as directly as possible by elected trustees or commissioners. In the case of the National Public Banking, perhaps the most logical of natural monopolies, unearned income is squeezed out of the system by fixing the interest rate at 1%. The concentration of monetary power is dissolved by distributing its essential function—the creation of money—to local communities.

***

To sum up, for most early Americans as a practical matter, and for radical populists as a theoretical matter, the measure of wealth was not income, but rather assets which could be put to work to produce income. The frontier vision promoted the idea of a right to ownership of productive assets, and to the benefits which can be realized from them. With the triumph and consolidation of centralized private banking in the United States after 1896, with its credit and debt monopoly grip over the economy, and the associated rise of corporate power and industrial labor, the idea of an individual right to productive assets gradually vanished. Unbacked fiat money schemes today ignore the right to assets in favor of a right to income. The struggle today is over the distribution of income, and not, as it should be, over the distribution of assets, particularly claims to assets, or money.

The populist proposal of a right to claim productive property in our time means the right to credit, since credit remains indispensable to the acquisition and utilization of assets. Credit is itself an asset, if employed productively. The frontier is long gone, but the right to credit remains its legacy as the instrument by which actual assets are secured and developed. We can no longer find empty land to homestead, but we can still claim a right to credit, and to its full benefits. As a public right, credit cannot be monopolized and controlled by private interests. It must instead be guaranteed by the government equally to all citizens at a uniform and stable, non-usurious interest rate.

There is no reason why public banks in every community should not be empowered to create debt-money by lending to local citizens on a non-profit, non-usurious basis. This would literally put the power of money creation into the truest of all sovereign hands, the hands of the people, or natural persons, where it surely belongs. It would ensure an abundance of credit to finance productive enterprises, the very basis for sustaining the economy. It would promote monetary stability by coordinating the monetary creation and monetary destruction necessarily present in any system of loans and repayments. If sovereignty is to be truly popular, it must allow for the direct participation of natural persons, or citizens, in its exercise. What kind of money could be more just by that standard than one which holds its value by rising and falling with the issuance of loans and their repayment? What could be more direct than individual participation in the creation of money by taking out a loan—for a mortgage, a business, education, or any private reason? What could be a better standard of social justice than to provide such loans publicly and uniformly to qualified (collateral backed) borrowers as a social service at nominal interest? What could be more democratic?

NOTES

1. On Jefferson's ward republics and confederal system of government, see Adrian Kuzminski, *Fixing the System: A History of Populism, Ancient and Modern* (New York: Bloomsbury Academic, 2008), Appendix: Jefferson's Ward Republics, 155–70.

2. Edward Kellogg, *A New Monetary System: The Only Means of Securing the Respective Rights of Labor and Property and of Protecting the Public from Financial Revulsions* (New York: Burt Franklin, 1970 [1861]), 286.

3. Ibid., 286.

4. Ibid., 275.

5. See Adam Winkler, "'Corporations Are People' Is Built on an Incredible 19th-Century Lie: How a Farcical Series of Events in the 1880s Produced an Enduring and Controversial Legal Precedent," *The Atlantic*, March 5, 2018, https://www.theatlantic.com/business/archive/2018/03/corporations-people-adam-winkler/554852/.

6. See for example the nineteenth-century monetary reforms in Denmark marked by saving banks, cooperative commercial banks, and mortgage credit associations described in Gretchen Ritter, *Goldbugs and Greenbacks: The Antimonopoly Tradition and the Politics of Finance in America, 1865–1896* (Princeton: Princeton University Press, 1997), 273–76.

7.Christine Berry and Laurie Macfarlane, *A New Public Banking Ecosystem: A Report to the Labor Party Commissioned by the Communication Workers Union and the Democracy Collaborative* (London: The Labour Party, n.d.), https://labour.org.uk/wp-content/uploads/2019/03/Building-a-new-public-banking-ecosystem.pdf.

8. Ibid.

9. Ibid.

10. Ibid.

11. See Kun Duan, Plamen Ivanov, and Richard Werner, "Deciphering the Chinese Economic Miracle: The Resolution of an Age-Old Economists' Debate—and Its Central Role in Rapid Economic Development," *The Review of Political Economy*, published online April 27, 2023.

12. Ibid.

13. Ibid.

14. See Richard A. Werner, "Towards a New Monetary Paradigm: A Quantity Theorem of Disaggregated Credit, with Evidence from Japan," *Kredit und Kapital* 30, no. 2 (1997): 276–309, https://eprints.soton.ac.uk/36569/1/KK_97_Disaggregated_Credit.pdf; see also Werner's "Towards a New Research Programme on 'Banking

and the Economy'—Implications of the Quantity Theory of Credit for the Prevention and Resolution of Banking and Debt Crises," *International Review of Financial Analysis* 25 (December 2012): 1–17, https://eprints.soton.ac.uk/36569/1/KK_97_Disaggregated_Credit.pdf.

15. For a current snapshot of the role of the *Mittelstand* see Erika Solomon, "As Germany's Business Model Wobbles, Firms Reassess Reliance on China," *The New York Times*, July 7, 2023), https://www.nytimes.com/2023/07/06/world/europe/germany-china-business-economy.html.

16. Duan, Ivanov, and Werner, "Deciphering the Chinese Economic Miracle."

17. Ellen Brown, *Banking on the People: Democratizing Money in the Digital Age* (Washington: The Democracy Collaborative, 2019); see also The Public Banking Institute, https://publicbankinginstitute.org/.

18. Edward Kellogg, *Labor and Other Capital: The Rights of Each Secured and the Wrongs of Both Eradicated* (New York: Augustus M Kelley, 1971 [1849]), 37. Emphasis by Kellogg.

19. Ibid., 282–82.

Bibliography

Benes, Jaromir (See Kumhof, Michael).

Bentham, Jeremy. *Defense of Usury: Shewing the Impolicy of the Present Legal Restraints on the Terms of Pecuniary Bargains.* Liberty Fund: Library of Liberty [1787] https://oll.libertyfund.org/title/bentham-defence-of-usury.

Bernstein, Peter L. *A Primer on Money, Banking, and Gold.* New York: Vintage Books, 1965.

———. *Against the Gods: The Remarkable Story of Risk.* New York: John Wiley and Sons, 1998.

Berry, Christine, and Macfarlane, Laurie. *A New Public Banking Ecosystem: A Report to the Labor Party Commissioned by the Communication Workers Union and the Democracy Collaborative.* London: The Labour Party, n.d. https://labour.org.uk/wp-content/uploads/2019/03/Building-a-new-public-banking-ecosystem.pdf.

A Bill to Establish a System of Sub-Treasuries, and for Other Purposes. H. R. 7162, 1890 [The Sub-Treasury Act] reprinted in A. A. Dunning, *The Farmers Alliance History and Agricultural Digest*. London: Forgotten Books, 2012 [1891], 336–38.

Brown, Ellen. *The Web of Debt: The Shocking Truth About Our Money System.* Baton Rouge: Third Millenium Press, 2007.

———. *Banking on the People: Democratizing Money in the Digital Age.* Washington: The Democracy Collaborative, 2019.

Campbell, Alexander. *The True American System of Finance: The Rights of Labor and Capital, and the Common Sense Way of Doing Justice to the Soldiers and Their Families: No Banks, Greenbacks the Exclusive Currency*. Chicago: Evening Journal Book and Job Print, 1864 [Cornell University Library Digital Collections, 2014]. https://digital.library.cornell.edu/catalog/may906923.

Catton, Jr., William R. *Overshoot: The Ecological Basis of Revolutionary Change.* Urbana: University of Illinois Press, 1982.

Chen, James. *Debt and Economic Renewal in the Ancient Near East.* Michael Hudson and Marc Van De Mieroop, eds. Bethesda: CDL, 2002.

———. "Basel Accords: Purpose, Pillars, History and Member Countries." Investopedia, July 27, 2022. https://www.investopedia.com/terms/b/basel_accord.asp.

Dematos, Daniel. “Sumerian Loans.” *The Tontine Coffeehouse: A History of Finance*, November 28, 2022. https://tontinecoffeehouse.com/2022/11/28/sumerian-loans/.

Desan, Christine A. *Making Money: Coin, Currency, and the Coming of Capitalism*. Oxford: Oxford University Press, 2014.

Destler, Chester McArthur. *American Radicalism: 1865–1901*. Chicago: Quadrangle Books, 1966 [1946].

———. “The Influence of Edward Kellogg upon American Radicalism, 1865–1896.” *Journal of Political Economy* XL (June 1932): 338–65; reprinted in Chester McArthur Destler, *American Radicalism 1865–1901* Chicago: Quandrangle Books, 1966 [1946].

Dunning, A. A. *The Farmers Alliance History and Agricultural Digest*. London: Forgotten Books, 2012 [1891].

Feinig, Jakob. *Moral Economics of Money: Politics and the Monetary Constitution of Society.* Stanford: Stanford University Press, 2022.

Fisher, Irving, et al. “A Program for Monetary Reform,” July 1939. https://monetary.org/images/pdfs/a_program_for_monetary_reform.pdf.

“Fractional Reserve Banking and How It Works” Investopedia, December 2022. https://www.investopedia.com/terms/f/fractionalreservebanking.asp.

Galbraith, James K. “In Defense of Low Interest Rates.” Annandale-on-Hudson: Levy Economics Institute of Bard College: Policy Note, July 2023. https://www.levyinstitute.org/pubs/pn_23-3.pdf.

Goetzmann, William N. *Money Changes Everything: How Finance Made Civilization Possible*. Princeton: Princeton University Press, 2017.

Goodhart, Charles, and Meinhard Jensen. “Currency School versus Banking School: An Ongoing Confrontation.” *Economic Thought* 4, no. 2 (2015), 20–31. https://eprints.lse.ac.uk/64068/1/Currency%20School%20versus%20Banking%20School.pdf.

Goodwyn, Lawrence. *The Populist Moment: A Short History of the Agrarian Revolt in America*. Oxford: Oxford University Press, 1978.

Graeber, David. *Debt: The First 5,000 Years*. Brooklyn: Melville House, 2011.

Hensarlin, Jeb, and Michael Solon. “Regulators May Sink America’s Banks: A Credit-Tightening Increase on Capital Standards Won’t Help the American Economy.” *The Wall Street Journal*, June 22, 2023. https://www.wsj.com/articles/regulators-may-sink-americas-banks-credit-economy-federal-reserve-crisis-4ccf1dc?mod=opinion_lead_pos5.

Hicks, John D. *The Populist Revolt: A History of the Farmers’ Alliance and the People’s Party*. Lincoln, NE: University of Nebraska Press, 1961 [1931].

Hollis, Christopher. *The Two Nations: A Financial Study of English History*. New York: Gordon Press, 1975.

Homer, Sydney, and Richard Sylla. *A History of Interest Rates,* 3rd ed. Rutgers, Rutgers University Press, 1996.

Huber, Joseph. “Currency vs. Banking Teachings: A Frame of Reference of Lasting Relevance to Modern Money Systems.” Sovereign Money: Website for Monetary Systems Analysis and Reform, n.d. https://sovereignmoney.site/1-currency-versus-banking-teachings.

———. *Sovereign Money: Beyond Reserve Banking*. Cham: Palgrave Macmillan, 2017.

Hudson, Michael. . . . *And Forgive Them Their Debts: Lending, Foreclosure, and Redemption from Bronze Age Finance to the Jubilee Year*. Dresden: Islet-Verlag, 2018.

Jacobs, Jane. *The Death and Life of Great American Cities.* New York: Random House, 1992.

Kellogg, Edward. *A New Monetary System: The Only Means of Securing the Respective Rights of Labor and Property and of Protecting the Public from Financial Revulsions.* New York: Burt Franklin, 1970 [1861].

———. *Labor and Other Capital: The Rights of Each Secured and the Wrongs of Both Eradicated.* New York: Augustus Kelley, 1971 [1849].

———. [writing as "Whitehook"] "Remarks upon Usury and Its Effects: A National Bank a Remedy in a Letter. Etc." New York: Harper and Brothers, 1841. https://www.libertarian-labyrinth.org/from-the-archives/edward-kellogg-remarks-upon-usury/.

———. [writing as "Unknown Author"] *A Treatise of the Currency and the Exchanges: Proposing a Remedy for the Evils That Exist in Relation to Them, by the Establishment of a General Exchange Office, Which Shall Also Be the Fiscal Agent of Government*. New York: Hopkins and Jennings, 1841. https://books.google.je/books?id=4jgKAQAAMAAJ&printsec=frontcover#v=onepage&q&f=false.

Kelton, Stephanie. *The Deficit Myth: Modern Monetary Theory and the Birth of the People's Economy*. New York: Public Affairs, 2020.

Knapp, Georg Friedrich. *The State Theory of Money*. Mrs. Lucas, trans. London: Macmillan, 1924.

Kornai, Janos. *The Socialist System: The Political Economy of Communism.* Princeton: Princeton University Press: 1992.

Kumhof, Michael, and Jaromir Benes. "The Chicago Plan Revisited." International Monetary Fund: *IMF Working Papers*: Working Paper WP12/202, August 2012. https://www.imf.org/en/Publications/WP/Issues/2016/12/31/The-Chicago-Plan-Revisited-26178.

Kurke, Leslie. *Coins, Bodies, Games, and Gold.* Princeton: Princeton University Press, 1999.

Kuzminski, Adrian. *Fixing the System: A History of Populism, Ancient and Modern.* New York: Continuum Books, 2008.

———. *The Ecology of Money: Debt, Growth, and Sustainability.* Lanham: Lexington Books, 2013.

Leggett, William. *Democratick Editorials: Essays in Jacksonian Political Economy*. Lawrence H. White, ed. Indianapolis: Liberty Press, 1984.

Lewis, Nathan. "The BRICS Go for Gold." *Forbes*, July 16, 2023.

Lowenstein, Roger. *Ways and Means: Lincoln and His Cabinet and the Financing of the Civil War*. New York: Penguin Books, 2022.

Macfarlane, Laurie (see Berry, Christine).

Macmillan, Jonathan. *The End of Banking: Money, Credit, and the Digital Revolution.* Zurich: Zero/One Economics, 2014.

Martenson, Chris. *The Crash Course: The Unsustainable Future of Our Economy, Energy, and Environment*. Hoboken: John Wiley & Sons, 2011.

McLeay, Michael, et al. "Money Creation in the Modern Economy." Bank of England. *Quarterly Bulletin* Q1 (2014), 14–27.

McMath, Robert C. Jr., *American Populism: A Social History 1877–1898*. New York: Hill and Wang, 1993.

Meadows, Donella, et al. *The Limits to Growth: The 30 Year Update*. White River Junction: Chelsea Green Publishing, 2004.

Meinhard, Jensen (see Goodhart, Charles).

Mendenhall, Thomas. *An Entire New Plan for a National Currency; Suited to the Demands of this Great, Improving, Agricultural, Manufacturing and Commercial Republic, to which Is Added a Plan for a Real National Bank*. Philadelphia: J. Rackstraw, 1834. https://archive.org/details/newplanfornation0000thom&view=theater.

Mitchell, Wesley C. "The Value of 'Greenbacks' during the Civil War." *Journal of Political Philosophy* 6, no. 2 (March 1898): 139–67.

Mogan, W. Scott. "Overproduction—the Law of Supply and Demand." In *A Populist Reader: Selections from the Works of American Populist Leaders*. George Brown Tindall, ed. New York: Harper & Row, 1966.

Mosler, Warren B. *Seven Deadly Innocent Frauds of Economic Policy.* St. Croix, U.S. V.I.: Valence Co., 2010.

———. *Soft Currency Economics.* West Palm Beach, FL: Adams, Viner and Mosler, 1995. https://web.archiv.org/web/20060904234833/http://epicoalition.org:80/docs/soft0004.htm.

The National Emergency Employment Defense Act of 2011 H. R. 2990 [The NEED Act]. https://www.congress.gov/bill/112th-congress/house-bill/2990.

Nevil, Scott. *The Omaha Platform*. Reprinted in *A Populist Reader*, George Brown Tindall, ed. *Selections from the Works of American Populist Leaders*. New York: Harper & Row, 1966, 90–96.

Norman Pollock. *A Populist Reader: Selections from the Works of American Populist Leaders*. George B. Tindall ed. New York: Harper and Row, 1966.

———. *The Populist Response to Industrial America: Midwestern Populist Thought.* New York: Norton Library, 1966.

Proudhon, Pierre-Joseph. *The Solution of the Social Problem* [Excerpts]. The Anarchist Library, 2012, Part IV, "The Bank of Exchange." https://theanarchistlibrary.org/library/pierre-joseph-proudhon-the-solution-of-the-social-problem.

Public Banking Institute. https://publicbankinginstitute.org/.

Reisen, Dominick J. *Middlefield and the Settling of the New York Frontier*. Voorheesville: Square Circle Press, 2009.

Sebag, Roy. *The Natural Order of Money*. White River Junction: Chelsea Green Publishing, 2022.

Simpson, C, V. J. "The German Sparkassen: A Commentary and Case Study." London: Simpson Associates, January 2013. http://www.civitas.org.uk/content/files/SimpsonSparkassen.pdf.

Soddy, Frederick. *Wealth, Virtual Wealth and Debt: The Solution of the Economic Paradox*. Palmdale: Omni Publications, 1983.

Solomon, Erika. "As Germany's Business Model Wobbles, Firms Reassess Reliance on China." *The New York Times*, July 7, 2023. https://www.nytimes.com/2023/07/06/world/europe/germany-china-business-economy.html.

Solon, Michael (see Hensarlin, Jeb).

Solon, Michael. "State of Small Business Now." U.S. Chamber of Commerce, April 2023. https://www.uschamber.com/small-business/state-of-small-business-now.

"Sparkassen Savings Banks in Germany." *Centre For Public Impact: A BCG Foundation*, March 2, 2017. https://www.centreforpublicimpact.org/case-study/sparkassen-savings-banks-germany.

Sutela, Pekka. "Monetary System, Soviet." Encyclopedia.com, February 2023. https://www.encyclopedia.com/history/encyclopedias-almanacs-transcripts-and-maps/monetary-system-soviet.

Sylla, Richard (see Homer, Sydney).

Teitelbaum, Richard. "Conspiracy Theorists Ask 'Who Owns the New York Fed?' Here's the Answer." Institutional Investor, February 24, 2020. https://www.institutionalinvestor.com/article/b1kh4p10qysrhv/Conspiracy-Theorists-Ask-Who-Owns-the-New-York-Fed-Here-s-the-Answer.

Tocqueville, Alexis de. *Democracy in America*. Henry Reeve, trans. Vols. I and II. New York: Bantam Books, 2002.

Turner, Frederick Jackson. *The Significance of the Frontier in American History*. Mansfield Center: Martino Publishing, 2014 [1894].

Tye, Robert. *Gyges' Magic Ring? The Origins of Coinages and Open Societies*. York: Published by Robert Tye, revised version, 2013, New Preface, 2022. https://www.academia.edu/356701/Gyges_Magic_Ring_The_Origin_of_Coinages_and_Open_Societies_2022_update.

Ungar, Irwin. *The Greenback Era: A Social and Political History of American Finance, 1865–1879*. Princeton: Princeton University Press, 1964.

Van De Mieroop, Marc (See Hudson, Michael, under Chen, James).

Werner, Richard A. "Towards a New Monetary Paradigm: A Quantity Theory of Disaggregated Credit." *Kredit und Kapital* 30, no. 2 (1997): 276–309 https://eprints.soton.ac.uk/36569/1/KK_97_Disaggregated_Credit.pdf.

Werner, Richard A. "Towards a New Research Programme on 'Banking and The Economy'—Implications of the for the Prevention and Resolution of Banking and Debt Crises." *International Review of Financial Analysis* 25 (2012): https://eprints.soton.ac.uk/36569/1/KK_97_Disaggregated_Credit.pdf

———. et al. *Where Does Money Come From? A Guide to the UK Monetary and Banking System*. 2nd ed. London: New Economics Foundation, 2012.

———. "Can Banks Individually Create Money Out of Nothing?—The Theories and the Empirical Evidence." *International Review of Financial Analysis* 36 (2014), 1–19.

———. "How Do Banks Create Money, and Why Can Other Firms Not Do the Same? An Explanation for the Coexistence of Lending and Deposit Taking." *International Review of Financial Analysis* 36 (2014): 71–77.

———. “A Lost Century of Economics: Three Theories of Banking and the Conclusive Evidence.” *International Review of Financial Analysis* 46 (July 2016): 361–79.

———. “Central Banks Are Too Powerful . . .” *Fortune: Conversation Insights*, March 20, 2023. https://fortune.com/2023/03/20/is-federal-reserve-too-powerful-inflation-quantitative-easing-richard-werner/.

——— et al. “Deciphering the Chinese Economic Miracle: The Resolution of an Age-old Economists' Debate–and its Central Role in Rapid Economic Development” *Review of Political Economy*, April 27, 2023. https://www.tandfonline.com/doi/full/10.1080/09538259.2023.2180200.

Whitten, David O. “The Depression of 1893.” Economic History

Association, EH-net. https://eh.net/?s=Whitten.

Winkler, Adam. “‘Corporations Are People’ Is Built on an Incredible 19th-Century Lie: How a Farcical Series of Events in the 1880s Produced an Enduring and Controversial Legal Precedent.” *The Atlantic*, March 5, 2018. https://www.theatlantic.com/business/archive/2018/03/corporations-people-adam-winkler/554852/.

Wray, L. Randall. *Modern Money Theory: A Primer on Macroeconomics for Sovereign Monetary Systems*, 2nd ed. London: Palgrave Macmillan, 2015.

———. “Modern Monetary Theory for Beginners.” YouTube, April 25, 2018, 37 minute mark. https://www.youtube.com/watch?v=E5JTn7GS4oA.

Zarlenga, Stephen. *The Lost Science of Money: The Mythology of Money—the Story of Power*. Valatie: American Monetary Institute, 2002.

Further Readings

Andreau, Jean. *Banking and Business in the Roman World*. Janet Lloyd, trans. Cambridge: Cambridge University Press, 1999.

Bagehot, Walter. *Lombard Street: A Description of the Money System*. Revised ed. London: White Crane, 2017.

Board of Governors of the Federal Reserve System. *The Federal Reserve System: Purposes and Functions*. 10th ed. Washington: Board of Governors of the Federal Reserve System, 2016.

Bodenhorn, Howard. *State Banking in Early America: A New Economic History*. Oxford: Oxford University Press, 2003.

Borsodi, Ralph. *Inflation and the Coming Keynesian Catastrophe: The Story of the Exeter Experiments with Constants*. Great Barrington: E. F. Schumacher Society, 1989.

Bowes, Robert. "Monetary Reform: PBI, AMI, the Green New Deal—Taking It to the Next Level." Colorado Public Banking, 2014.

Buchan, James. *Frozen Desire: The Meaning of Money*. New York: Welcome Rain, 1997.

Cantrell, Gregg. *The People's Revolt: Texas Populists and the Roots of American Liberalism*. New Haven: Yale University Press, 2007.

Carruthers, Bruce G. *City of Capital: Politics and Markets in the English Financial Revolution*. Princeton: Princeton University Press, 1996.

Casu, Barbara, et al. *Introduction to Banking*. Harlow: Prentice Hall, 2006.

Del Mar, Alexander. *History of Monetary Systems*. Chicago: Charles J. Kerr Company, 1896.

———. *The History of Money in America: From the Earliest Times to the Establishment of the Constitution*. Hawthorne Publications, 1979 [1899].

Desan, Christine A. "How to Spend a Trillion Dollars: Our Monetary Hardwiring, Why it Matters, and What to Do about It." Harvard Public Law Working Paper, No. 22–04, 2022 https://papers.ssrn.com/sol3/papers.cfm?abstract_id=4056241.

Dickson, P. G. M. *The Financial Revolution in England: A Study in the Development of Public Credit 1688–1756*. London: Macmillan, 1967.

Di Muzio, Tim, and Noble, Leonie. "The Coming Revolution in Political Economy: Money Creation, Mankiw and Misguided Macroeconomics,"" pp. 85–108. *Real World Economics Review*, no. 80 (2017).

Douthwaite, Richard. *The Ecology of Money*. Bristol: Green Book Limited, 1999.

Ehrenberg, Richard. *Capital and Finance in the Age of the Renaissance: A Study of the Fuggers and their Connections*. H. M. Lucas, trans. Fairfield: Augustus Kelley 1985 [1928].

Ferguson, Niall. *The Cash Nexus: Money and Power in the Modern World, 1700–2000.* New York: Basic Books, 2001.

———. *Financial Structure and Economic Growth: A Cross-Country Comparison of Banks, Markets, and Development*. Asli Demirguc-Kunt and Ross Levine, eds. Cambridge: MIT Press, 2004.

———. *The Ascent of Money: A Financial History of the World*. New York: Penguin Books, 2008.

Galbraith, John Kenneth. *Money: Whence It Came, Where It Went.* Boston: Houghton Mifflin Company, 1975

Garrett, Garet. *A Bubble That Broke the World.* Boston: Little Brown and Company, 1932.

Garrett, Garet, and Murray N. Rothbard. *The Great Depression and New Deal Monetary Policy*. San Francisco: Cato Institute, 1980.

Gause, Andrew. *The Secret World of Money*. Hilton Head Island: SDL Press, 1996.

Goodwin, Jason. *Greenback: The Almighty Dollar and the Invention of America*. New York: Henry Holt and Company, 2003.

Greco, Jr., Thomas H. *Money and Debt: A Solution to the Global Crisis*. 2nd ed. Tucson: Thomas J Greco, Jr., 1990.

———. *Money: Understanding and Creating Alternatives to Legal Tender*. White River Junction: Chelsea Green Publishing 2001.

Greider, William. *Secrets of the Temple: How the Federal Reserve Runs the Country.* New York: Simon and Schuster, 1987.

Griffin, G. Edward. *The Creature from Jekyll Island: A Second Look at the Federal Reserve*. 4th ed. West Lake Village: American Media, 2009.

Hacker, Andrew. *Money: Who Has How Much and Why*. New York: Touchstone Books, 1998.

Hayek, Friedrich A. *The Road to Serfdom*. Chicago: University of Chicago Press, 1944.

Hixon, William F. *A Matter of Interest: Reexamining Money, Debt, and Real Economic Growth*. Montgomery: E-Book Time, 1991.

———. *Triumph of the Bankers: Money and Banking in the Eighteenth and Nineteenth Centuries*. Montgomery: E-Book Time 1993.

Hockett, Robert C., and Saul T. Omarova. "The Finance Franchise." Ithaca: Cornell Law School, *Legal Studies Research Studies Series,* No. 16–29 (2017): https://papers.ssrn.com/sol3/papers.cfm?abstract_id=2820176.

Huber, Joseph. "Critical Remarks on R. Werner's Typology of Banking Theories." In *Sovereign Money: Website for Monetary System Analysis and Reform*. https://sovereignmoney.site/werner-typology-of-banking-theories.

———. "Modern Monetary Theory and New Currency Theory: A Comparative Discussion, Including an Assessment of Their Relevance to Monetary Reform." *Real World Economics Review*, no. 66 (2014): pp. 38–57.

Hudson, Michael. *The Bubble and Beyond: Fictitious Capital, Debt Deflation, and the Global Crisis*. Dresden: Islet, 2012.

Ihrig, Jane, and Scott A. Wolla. "The Fed's New Monetary Policy Tools." Federal Reserve Bank of St. Louis: *Econ Primer*, August 2020.

Ingham, Geoffrey. *The Nature of Money.* Cambridge: Polity Press, 2004.

Innis, A. Mitchell. "What Is Money?" *The Banking Law Journal* (May 1913): 377–408.

———. "The Credit Theory of Money" *The Banking Law Journal* 31 (December/January 1914):151–68.

Jevons, W. Stanley. *Money and the Mechanism of Exchange.* New York: D. Appleton, 1875 [Cornell University Library Digital Collections, 2010].

Kennedy, Margrit. *Interest and Inflation Free Money: Creating an Exchange Medium That Works for Everybody and Protects the Earth*. Okemos: Seva International, 1995.

———. *Occupy Money: Creating an Economy Where Everybody Wins*. Gabriola Island: New Society Publishers, 2012.

Keynes, John Maynard. *The General Theory of Employment, Interest, and Money.* New York: Houghton, Mifflin, Harcourt, 2016 [1936].

Kim, Jongchul. "The London Goldsmith-Bankers Institutionalization of Trust." York University, ms., n.d.

———. "Money Is Rights in Rem: A Note on the Nature of Money." *Journal of Economic Issues* (November 9, 2014):
https://papers.ssrn.com/sol3/papers.cfm?abstract_id=2520870.

Kumhof, Michael, et al. "Central Bank Money: Liability, Asset, or Equity of the Nation" Ithaca: Cornell Law School, *Legal Studies Research Studies Series*, No. 20–46 (2020): http://ssrn.com/abstract=3730608.

Kurland, Norman G., et al. *Capital Homesteading for Every Citizen: A Just Free Market Solution for Saving Social Security*. Washington: Center for Economic and Social Justice, 2004.

Kurtzman, Joel. *The Death of Money: How the Electronic Economy has Destabilized the World's Markets and Created Financial Chaos*. Boston: Little Brown, 1993.

Lanchester, John. "The Invention of Money: In Three Centuries, the Heresies of Two Bankers Became the Basis of Our Modern Economy," *The New Yorker*, July 29, 2019.

Law, John. *Money and Trade Considered: With a Proposal for Supplying the Nation with Money.* D. K. Narciedies, ed. Independently published: 2021 [1705].

———. *Essay on a Land Bank*. D. K. Narciedies, ed. Independently published, 2022 [circa 1705].

Lawson, Alfred. *Direct Credits for Everybody. Showing How Capitalism Will Work*. Detroit: Humanity Publishing Company, 1933.

Lazzarato, Maurizio. *The Making of the Indebted Man: An Essay on the Neoliberal Tradition*. Joshua David Jordan, trans. Amsterdam: semiotext(e), 2011.

Leavitt, Samuel. *Our Money Wars: The Example and Warning of American Finance*. Boston: Arena Publishing, 1894 [Cornell University Library Digital Collections, 2014].

Michener, Ron. “Money in the American Colonies” EH.net (Economic History Association, n.d.). https://eh.net/encyclopedia/money-in-the-american-colonies/.

Minsky, Hyman P. “Financial Instability and the Decline (?) of Banking: Public Policy Implications” Jerome Levy Economics Institute of Bard College: Working Paper, No. 127, 1994.

The Money Changers: Currency Reform from Aristotle to E-cash. David Boyle, ed. London: Earthscan Publications, 2002.

Modern Monetary Theory and Its Critics. Edward Fullbrook and Jamie Morgan, eds. Bristol: World Economics Association, 2019.

Morton, Frederic. *The Rothschilds: A Family Portrait.* London: Secker and Warburg. 1962.

Mullins, Eustace. *The Secrets of the Federal Reserve: The London Connection.* Staunton: Bankers Research Institute, 1993.

Neal, Larry. *The Rise of Financial Capitalism: International Capital Markets in the Age of Reason*. Cambridge: Cambridge University Press, 1993.

Nelson, Benjamin. *The Idea of Usury from Tribal Brotherhood to Universal Otherhood*. 2nd ed. Chicago: University of Chicago Press, 1969.

Noble, Leonie (see Di Muzio, Tim).

Omarova, Saul T. (see also Hockett, Robert C.).

Omarova, Saul T. “The People’s Leger: How to Democratize Money and Finance the Economy.” *Vanderbilt Law Review* 74, no. 5 (October 2021): 1231–1300.

Pash, Mark S. *Creating a 21st Century Win-Win Economy: The Problems and the Solutions*. Encino: Center for Progressive Economics, 2016.

Phillips, Ronnie J. *The Chicago Plan and New Deal Banking Reform*. Armonk: M. E. Sharpe, 1990.

Pozsar, Zoltan, et al. “Shadow Banking.” New York: Federal Reserve Bank of New York, Staff Report 458, revised, February 2012.

Quigley, Carroll. *Tragedy and Hope: A History of the World in Our Time*. New York: Macmillan, 1966.

Reigel, E. C. *Flight from Inflation: The Monetary Alternative*. Los Angeles: The Heather Foundation, 1978.

Ricardo, David. *The Principles of Political Economy and Taxation.* London: Everyman’s Library, 1973.

Roseveare, Henry. *The Financial Revolution: 1660–1760*. London: Longman, 1991.

Rothbard, Murray N. (see also Garrett, Garet).

Rothbard, Murray N.. *A History of Money and Banking in the United States: The Colonial Era to World War II*. Auburn: Ludwig von Mises Institute, 2002.

Sahr, Aaron. *Keystroke Capitalism: How Banks Create Money for the Few*. Sharon Howe, trans. London: Verso, 2022.

Schnacht, Hjalmar Horace Greeley. *Confessors of “The Old Wizard”: The Autobiography of Hjalmar Horace Greeley Schacht*. Diana Pyke, trans. Boston: Houghton Mifflin, 1956.

Search, R. E. *Lincoln Money Martyred*. Palmsdade: Omni Publications, 1989.
Shannon, Fred A. "C. W. Macune and the Farmers' Alliance." *Current History* 24 (June 1955): 330–35.
Simmel, Georg. *The Philosophy of Money.* Tom Bottomore and David Frisby, trans. London: Routledge & Kegan Paul, 1978.
Sklansky, Jeffrey. *Sovereign of the Market: The Money Question in Early America*. Chicago: University of Chicago Press, 2017.
Spooner, Lysander. *Our Financiers: Their Ignorance, Usurpations and Frauds*. Boston: A Williams & Co., 1877. https://en.wikisource.org/wiki/Our_Financiers:_Their_Ignorance,_Usurpations_and_Frauds.
Turnbull, Shann. *Democratising the Wealth of Nations from New Money Sources and Profit Motives*. Sydney: The Company Directors Association, 2000.
Tymoigne, Eric. "Seven Replies to the Critique of Modern Monetary Theory." Annandale-on-Hudson: Levy Economics Institute, Working Paper 996, December 2021.
Tymoigne, Eric, and L. Randall Wray. "Money: An Alternative Story." Center for Full Employment and Price Stability: Working Paper No. 45, July 2005.
Vilar, Pierre. *A History of Gold and Money: 1450 to 1920*. London: Verso, 1976.
Von Mises, Ludwig. *The Theory of Money and Credit*. H. E. Batson, trans. Indianapolis: Liberty Classics, 1980.
White, Andrew Dickson. *Fiat Money Inflation in France*. New York: Foundation for Economic Education, 1959.
White, Lawrence H. *Free Banking in Britain: Theory, Experience, and Debate,* 1800–1846.
Wolla, Scott A. (see Ihrig, Jane).
Wood, John H. *Money: Its Origins, Development, Debasement, and Prospects*. Great Barrington: American Institute for Economic Research, 1999.
Wray, L. Randall [see also Tymoigne, Eric].
Wray, L. Randall. *Modern Money Theory: A Primer on Macroeconomics for Sovereign Monetary Systems.* 2nd ed. New York: Palgrave Macmillan, 2015.
Wright, Robert E. *Origins of Commercial Banking in America, 1750–1800*. Lanham: Rowman & Littlefield, 2001.

Index

About the Author

Adrian Kuzminski writes on political and philosophical issues. His works include *Fixing the System: A History of Populism, Ancient and Modern* (2008), *The Ecology of Money: Debt, Growth, and Sustainability* (2013), *Pyrrhonism: How the Ancient Greeks Reinvented Buddhism* (2008), and *Pyrrhoniam Buddhism* (2021). He lives in rural upstate New York.